ATTACK ON PEARL HARBOR

AMERICA ENTERS WORLD WAR II

Peter Darman, Editor

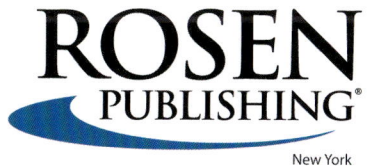

ROSEN
PUBLISHING®

New York

This edition is published in 2013 by:

The Rosen Publishing Group, Inc.
29 East 21st Street, New York, NY 10010

For Brown Bear Books Ltd:
Editorial Director: Lindsey Lowe
Senior Editor: Tim Cooke
Military Editor: Pete Darman
Children's Publisher: Anne O'Daly
Art Director: Jeni Child
Picture Manager: Sophie Mortimer

Library of Congress Cataloging-in-Publication Data

Darman, Peter.
  Attack on Pearl Harbor: America enters World War II/Peter Darman.
     p. cm.—(World War II)
Includes bibliographical references and index.
ISBN 978-1-4488-9233-4 (library binding)
1. Pearl Harbor (Hawaii), Attack on, 1941—Juvenile literature. 2. World War, 1939–1945—Causes—Juvenile literature. I. Title.
D767.92.D36 2013
940.54'26693—dc23
                                                                          2012017497

Manufactured in the United States of America

CPSIA Compliance Information: Batch #W13YA: For further information, contact Rosen Publishing, New York, at 1-800-237-9932

CONTENTS

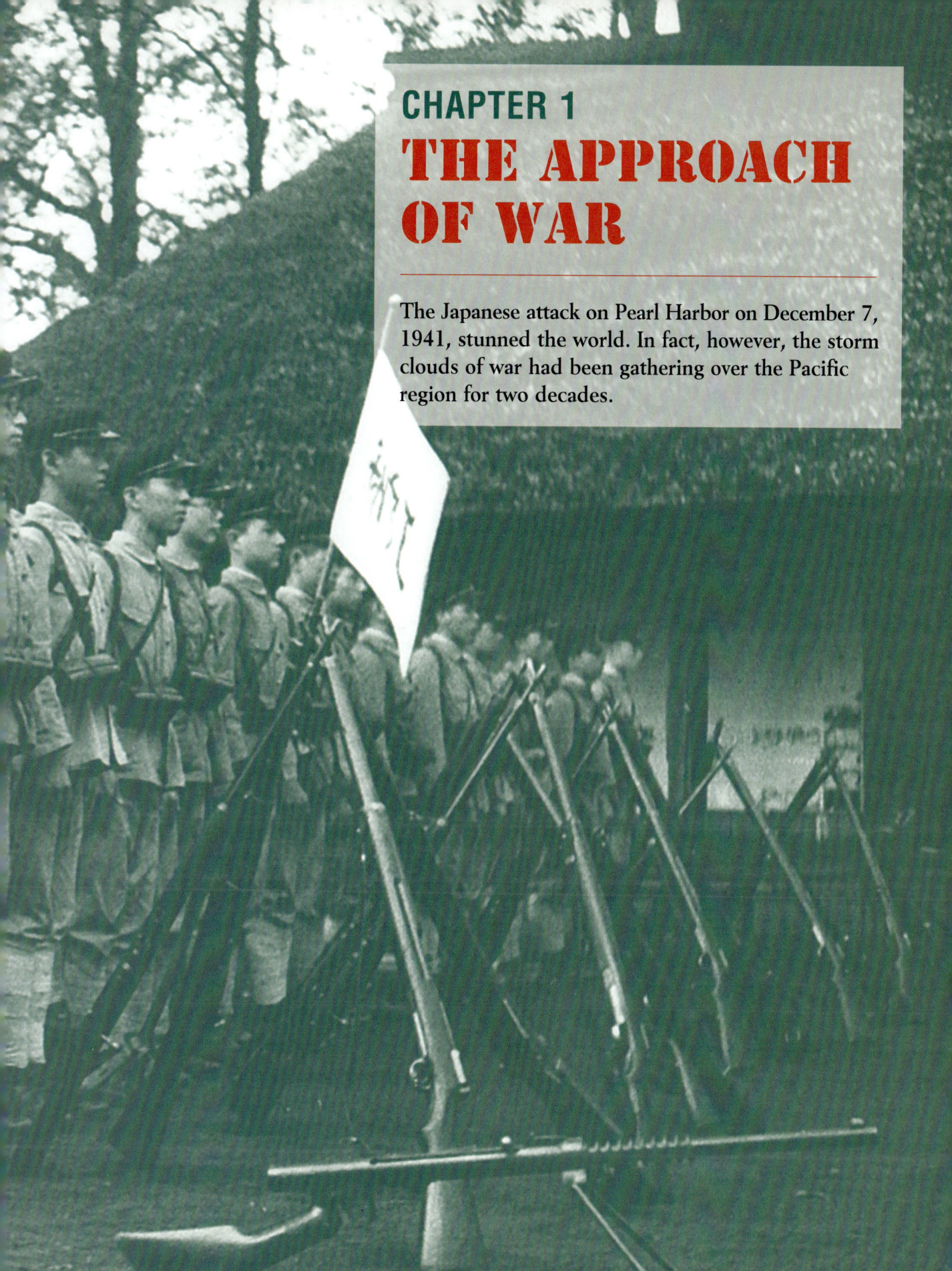

CHAPTER 1
THE APPROACH OF WAR

The Japanese attack on Pearl Harbor on December 7, 1941, stunned the world. In fact, however, the storm clouds of war had been gathering over the Pacific region for two decades.

Previous pages:
Students undergo military training in the 1930s. Their machine gun is adapted to fire only blank ammunition.

> "The United States and Britain felt threatened by Japan's growing power"

Japanese troops land at Hangchow Bay in eastern China on November 5, 1937. Within weeks the invasion brought several strategic cities on the Chinese mainland under Japanese control, including Beijing and Shanghai.

Japan had begun modernizing in 1867. Reformers overthrew the old government in the so-called Meiji Restoration. They ended centuries of international isolation. They set up a new government and began industrial development modeled on Western lines. The Japanese also began a program of expansion. They needed resources to support their industrial growth. In the latter decades of the nineteenth century, Japan added numerous islands to its empire. It defeated China in the Sino-Japanese War (1894–1895). It showed its growing military strength again with a surprise defeat of Russia in the Russo-Japanese War (1904–1905). In 1910, Japan annexed the Korean peninsula.

In World War I (1914–1918), Japan backed the Western allies. It took control of German possessions in the Pacific and China. The 1919 Treaty of Versailles confirmed Japan's gains. They included the Palau, Caroline, and Marshall islands and part of the Marianas. Japan also kept control of Germany's former territories in northeast China, to the great resentment of the Chinese.

By 1919, Japanese ambitions had aroused the suspicion of the colonial powers in the region. Britain possessed Malaya, Burma, Singapore, and Hong Kong. The French controlled French Indochina and the Dutch East Indies. United States Pacific territories included Hawaii, Guam, and the Philippines.

The United States and Britain felt threatened by Japan's growing power. They were alarmed by Japan's ambitions

in China, particularly after the Twenty-One Demands of 1915. The demands tried to bring China and its vast resources under Japanese control. It also became clear after 1919 that Japan was less interested in acting as a guardian of its new territories, as mandated by the League of Nations, than in exploiting their resources for industrial growth.

Long-standing tensions

There were other causes of tension between Japan and the United States. One related to Japanese immigration. In the late nineteenth and the early twentieth century, thousands of Japanese moved to the United States. They were mainly looking for work in industries on the West Coast. Their arrival prompted a racist reaction from many Americans. They believed that the immigrants were stealing jobs and lowering wages. An 1894 treaty gave Japanese citizens the right to enter and work in the United States. The U.S. government began to enforce a clause in the treaty forbidding immigration that took jobs away from U.S. citizens. The Japanese feeling that the Western powers treated them as inferior was reinforced during the Russo–Japanese War. United States president Theodore Roosevelt

This Japanese painting shows the Battle of Tsushima in May 1905. Japan's victory over Russia was the first time in the modern period that an Asian power had defeated a European power in a naval battle.

Priests protest against unemployment in Tokyo in the mid-1920s. A huge earthquake in September 1923 worsened the state of the Japanese economy.

helped broker a peace deal, but the Japanese believed that they did not gain the full rewards for their victory. They blamed the United States. The Japanese felt a similar sense of grievance after the Treaty of Versailles. Again, they believed that their gains were less than those of the other victorious powers.

Japan had defeated the Russian fleet at the Battle of Tsushima in May 1905. It was the first naval defeat by an Asian power of a Western power in the modern period. Japan continued its naval expansion after World War I. The United States and Britain were the chief naval powers in the Pacific. Their interests would be threatened by a powerful Japanese Navy. In 1921 and 1922, they held a series of conferences in Washington, D.C. The talks aimed to stabilize the naval balance in the Pacific. The Washington Naval Treaty of 1922 placed restrictions on the tonnage of battleships, aircraft carriers, and cruisers that Japan could build in relation to those of the United States and Britain. The ratio was fixed at 5:5:3 for the United States, Britain, and Japan respectively. The United States and Britain argued that they had naval commitments outside the Pacific, so the Japanese would effectively have equal forces in the Pacific.

Anti-Western feelings

The Japanese came to see the treaty as a source of national humiliation. It was followed by the 1924 Immigration Act. The act stopped all Japanese immigration to the United States, as well as that of other nationalities, particularly from Asia. The Japanese again found the act humiliating.

The Japanese sense of international humiliation had an impact on politics at home. The 1910s and 1920s were a generally liberal period in Japan. Western music and fashions became popular among young, urban Japanese. However, many conservatives resented what they saw as Japan's humiliation. Many of them belonged to the military. They thought that the country should turn back to its traditional values. Those values were best summed up by Japan's historic knights, the samurai.

In 1921, a fanatic militarist stabbed to death Japan's moderate prime minister, Takashi Hara. Meanwhile, former soldiers became important members of youth groups, particularly in rural parts of the country. The veterans instilled their militaristic values into young people.

Despite the rise in militarism, politics remained largely liberal. In 1926, Emperor Hirohito came to the throne. He was seen as being pro-Western. Japan also continued to develop a modern economy.

Japan's prosperity was crippled by a banking collapse in 1927 and the onset of the worldwide Great Depression in 1929. At the same time, the country's population had nearly doubled in size to 56 million in the 50 years before 1920. It had outstripped its supply of natural resources. Most oil, coal, rubber, and metals had to be imported; the United States provided 60 percent of Japan's oil. For Japan's militarists, such dependency was a further blow to national pride.

> "One of the main reasons Japan went to war in 1941 was to try to guarantee its access to natural resources"

Economic hardship

One of the main reasons Japan went to war in 1941 was to try to guarantee its access to natural resources. Militarists began to argue for aggressive expansion to acquire the raw materials the country needed. They targeted an area that already lay within Japan's sphere of interest: Manchuria in northern China. The Japanese had acquired trading rights and concessions in the region since 1905. By the late 1920s, Japan controlled the South Manchuria Railroad and exploited Manchuria's natural resources.

THE KWANTUNG ARMY

Also known as the Guandong Army, the Kwantung Army was a regular formation of the Imperial Japanese Army. It was stationed in Kwantung province in Manchuria. It began as a small garrison deployed to the Kwantung Leased Territory, which was a Japanese-controlled region. The garrison defended Japan's commercial interests and protected traffic along the South Manchuria Railroad. In 1919, the garrison was renamed as an army. Its 10,000 troops included an army division, an artillery battalion, and six battalions on railroad guard duties.

In 1931, the Kwantung Army faked a bombing on a train. It then occupied the whole of Manchuria. The Kwantung Army would remain in Manchuria and northern China until the end of World War II, rising to a peak strength of around 700,000 men. However, once the wider conflict broke out, thousands of its soldiers found themselves redeployed to the Pacific theater. The Kwantung Army finally surrendered to the Russians following the Soviet advance into Manchuria in August 1945.

The Kwantung Army grew from a small garrison to become the fearsome formation that occupied Manchuria in 1931.

The Japanese military increasingly acted outside government control. The army was somewhat more radical than the navy. Army commanders had become used to acting on their own authority at the end of World War I. They had been involved in civil wars in both Russia and China. In 1931, the Imperial Army invaded Manchuria. Its commanders had no authorization from the government. They calculated that Tokyo would have to approve the invasion once it had happened.

The hardliners gain control

The immediate justification for the invasion was an explosion on the Japanese-controlled South Manchuria Railroad on September 18, 1931. The bomb was almost certainly planted by the Japanese, but they blamed Chinese terrorists and invaded. Weakened by civil wars, the Chinese could not resist. By February 1932, the Kwantung Army had taken over Manchuria, which was renamed Manchukuo. For the next five years the Kwantung Army steadily pushed south. It extended its occupation to just north of the Chinese capital, Beijing.

At home, it became increasingly difficult to oppose the army. The militarists won more political power. Extremists assassinated two prime ministers, in 1930 and 1932. In 1933, after international condemnation of the invasion of Manchuria, Japan withdrew from the League of Nations. An attempted military coup in February 1936 failed. The government, however, was dominated by militarists who advocated aggressive territorial expansion.

In 1932, Japan had rejected the limitations of the Washington Naval Treaty. In 1937, it began building the

A convoy of trucks delivers supplies and additional troops for the advancing Kwantung Army in Manchuria in 1931. By February 1932, the region was wholly under the control of the Japanese.

EMPEROR HIROHITO

Although Emperor Hirohito bears some of the blame for the Pacific War, he was in many ways a puppet of the military factions that took over Japan in the 1920s and 1930s. Born on April 29, 1901, he grew into an open-minded and intelligent young man. As a young prince, he traveled to Europe in 1921. He showed more pro-Western tendencies than many of his countrymen. Following his father's death, he became Japan's emperor in 1926. He would hold the position for more than 60 years, making him Japan's longest-reigning monarch. Hirohito was not an aggressive warmaker. In 1931 he was highly critical of the military takeover of Manchuria. There is also evidence to show that he opposed Japanese alliances with Germany and Italy through the Tripartite Pact. Furthermore, although Hirohito gave his approval for the Pearl Harbor attack in 1941, he does not appear to have been enthusiastic for war with the United States. The fact that the war did occur shows the extent to which Hideki Tojo, the prime minister, was the true center of power in Japan. On August 15, 1945, after the dropping of atomic bombs on Hiroshima and Nagasaki, Hirohito made a radio address to the Japanese people. He announced Japan's surrender. The Allies did not prosecute Hirohito for war crimes. He lived quietly as emperor until his death in 1989.

world's largest battleships, the *Musashi* and *Yamato*. The military's policies enjoyed wide support among civilians.

By that time the Japanese had also negotiated the Anti-Comintern Pact (1936) with Germany. The pact was later extended to include Italy. The agreement was ostensibly aimed at limiting the spread of communism. It created a defensive alliance against a possible Soviet attack.

China under attack

Japan's militarists launched a massive program of rearmament in the mid–1930s. As a result, the country's need for supplies of natural resources increased. Military planners sought them in China. In July 1937, Japanese and Chinese troops clashed at the Marco Polo Bridge near Beijing. The episode began the Second Sino Japanese War (there had been a previous war in 1894–1895).

China's Nationalist government was led by Chiang Kai-shek. It was fighting a civil war with communist forces. Much of northern China, meanwhile, was controlled by warlords. The Japanese rapidly occupied most of China's coastal territories and its main cities, including Beijing and Shanghai. Chiang's government fled Nanking shortly before the city fell in December. Japanese troops went on to massacre

Chinese, European, and U.S. civilians leave Nanking as the Japanese close in on the city in December 1937. China's Nationalist Army fled the city, leaving its citizens to face Japanese atrocities that became known as the "Rape of Nanking."

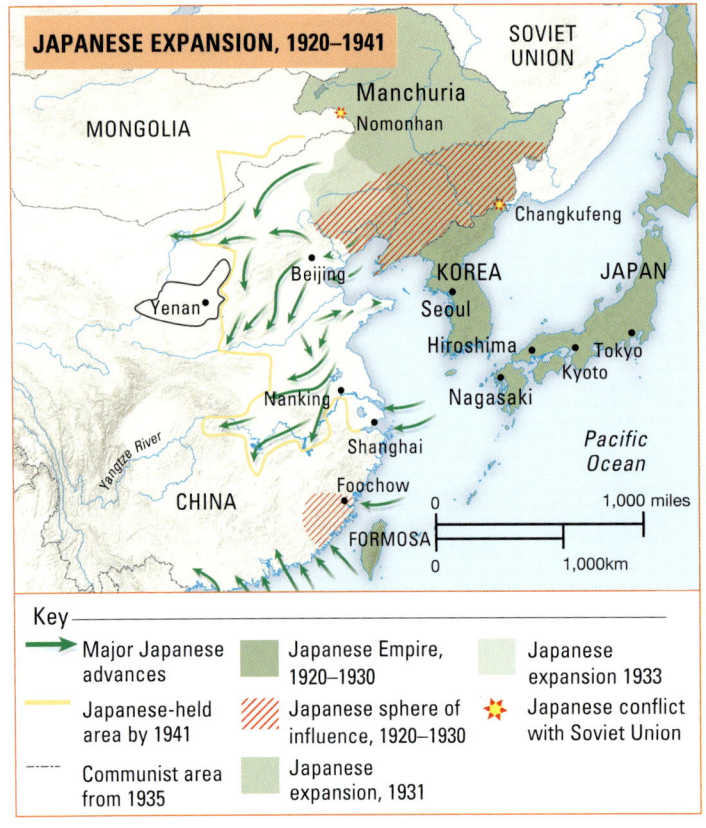

JAPANESE EXPANSION, 1920–1941

SOVIET UNION

MONGOLIA

Manchuria
Nomonhan

Changkufeng

KOREA
Beijing
Yenan
Seoul

JAPAN
Hiroshima
Tokyo
Kyoto

Nanking
Nagasaki

Shanghai

Pacific Ocean

Yangtze River

CHINA

Foochow

0   1,000 miles

FORMOSA

0   1,000km

Key

→ Major Japanese advances

Japanese Empire, 1920–1930

Japanese expansion 1933

Japanese-held area by 1941

Japanese sphere of influence, 1920–1930

✳ Japanese conflict with Soviet Union

----- Communist area from 1935

Japanese expansion, 1931

Japan's ambition to extend its empire into China met ineffective resistance from divided Chinese forces. It also led to two border clashes with the Soviet Union.

A Chinese family weep in the rubble of their house in Nanking, which was destroyed in a Japanese air raid on the city.

THE RAPE OF NANKING

The Rape of Nanking stands out as a notorious war crime even in a century of many atrocities against civilians. It occurred during the Second Sino-Japanese War. The war began on July 7, 1937, with the Japanese invasion of northern China. Nanking was the capital of China's Nationalist government. It had a population of around 700,000 (the numbers were swollen by war refugees). On December 7, as the Japanese closed in, the Nationalists fled. They left Nanking's citizens to their fate.

The Japanese assault on Nanking began on December 10 with huge air and artillery bombardments. By December 15, organized resistance had been crushed. Japanese soldiers began their occupation. In searching for Chinese troops mingling with the civilian population, Japanese troops embarked on nearly two months of unrestrained rape, torture, and murder. Japanese units held murder "competitions" to see who could cut off the most heads. They impaled children on bayonets and raped around 80,000 women, whom they usually murdered afterward. The killing was supported by the Japanese press.

The slaughter came to an end in February 1938. It was stopped partly to prevent the spread of disease from the many corpses. It also ended as a result of international outrage. Images and descriptions of the killings were smuggled out by Western journalists. In total, up to 200,000 people were killed. The massacre still sours Sino-Japanese relations.

more than 200,000 civilians in the city. In December 1937, Japanese aircraft sank the gunboat USS *Panay* on the Chang (Yangtze) River in China. The Japanese apologized. They blamed the attack on mistaken identity. The U.S. government, however, acted to curb the Japanese. It sent funds to the Chinese forces and also increased its own naval power in the Pacific.

Antagonizing the West

In the late 1930s and again in July 1940, the moderate Prince Konoe was the Japanese prime minister. Real power lay with militarists in his government, however. They included the war minister Hideki Tojo and the foreign minister Yosuke Matsuoka.

After Germany's defeat of France in the war in Europe in June 1940, Japan acquired military rights in Indochina. They set up bases there in return for acknowledging French sovereignty; the French authorities were in no position to resist. The Japanese military presence in Indochina threatened British interests in Burma and Malaya.

Dangerous alliances

On September 27, 1940, Matsuoka signed the Tripartite Pact with Germany and Italy. The agreement effectively committed the three to mutual defense in the event of an attack by the Soviet Union or the United States.

The Japanese government also unveiled its plan to create a "Greater East Asia Co-Prosperity Sphere." In theory, the strategy called for East Asia to rid itself of colonial influences and take over its own affairs. In reality, it was little more than a Japanese plan to control East Asia and the Pacific—and all of the region's resources.

In reaction to Japan's warlike moves, in July 1940 the U.S. Congress had

The Yamato, *here being fitted out in September 1941, was one of the largest battleships in the world when it was built.*

passed the Two Ocean Naval Expansion Act. The act began a program of warship production. Alarmed Japanese analysts calculated that, by 1944, the U.S. Navy would be more than three times the size of Japan's navy. For Japan to achieve military dominance of the Pacific, it would have to act fast.

In April 1941, Japan signed a non-aggression treaty with the Soviet Union. The treaty freed up much of its army. In

Eyewitness Report:

" The mass executions of war prisoners added to the horrors the Japanese brought to Nanking. After killing the Chinese soldiers who threw down their arms and surrendered, the Japanese combed the city for men in civilian garb... suspected of being former soldiers. Just before boarding the ship for Shanghai, the writer watched the execution of 200 men on the Bund (dike). The killings took 10 minutes. The men were lined against a wall and shot. Then a number of Japanese, armed with pistols, trod nonchalantly around the crumpled bodies, pumping bullets into any that were still kicking. The army men performing the gruesome job had invited navy men from the warships anchored off the Bund to view the scene. A large group of military spectators apparently greatly enjoyed the spectacle... I witnessed three mass executions of prisoners within a few hours. In one slaughter a tank gun was turned on a group of more than 100 soldiers at a bomb shelter near the Ministry of Communications. "

F. Tillman, reporter for *The New York Times*, Nanking, December 1937

THE JAPANESE NAVY

The Imperial Navy was perhaps the most striking symbol of Japan's rise to world power status during the first half of the twentieth century.

After the Meiji Restoration of 1867, Japan made a decisive shift toward re-creating itself on the model of a modern industrial power rather than trying to hang on to its old isolationist policy. In 1867 it already possessed eight modern warships and in July 1869 the Imperial Japanese Navy was formally established. Contacts were made with Britain, then the world's leading naval power, new warships were commissioned, and trainees were sent abroad (the first 14 to Britain) to learn the skills necessary for a modern naval power.

During the 1880s Japan also developed close relations with French shipbuilders. The result was that in the Sino–Japanese war of 1894–1895 its fleet easily destroyed the Chinese Navy. Even more stunning was the great naval victory over the Russians during the Russo–Japanese War of 1904–1905, during which Admiral Togo directed one of the great naval victories at Tsushima.

In the early years of the twentieth century Japan began to construct its own battleships and during World War I Japanese vessels contributed to the Allied war effort, including the deployment of a destroyer flotilla in the Mediterranean.

By the end of World War I the Japanese Navy was the world's third largest and also one of the most forward looking. In 1921, for example, the *Hosho* was the world's first purpose-built aircraft carrier to be launched. Such developments caused considerable alarm in the U.S. and Britain. Japan was forced to limit its naval forces by the Washington Treaty of 1922 and this caused great resentment. However, Japanese naval building still continued and the senior commanders of the navy continued to be receptive to new ideas—for example, inviting French and British military missions to demonstrate new aircraft and naval aviation tactics.

In 1941 the Japanese Navy consisted of 10 battleships, 10 aircraft carriers, 38 cruisers, 112 destroyers, and 65 submarines. The navy had developed an aggressive strategy, betting on winning decisive battles with ships that were better than those of its opponents: for example the *Yamato*, launched in 1941, was the largest and most heavily armed battleship ever built.

Right Japanese vessels attack the Russian naval base of Port Arthur during the Russo–Japanese War. The Russian Far East Fleet was effectively penned up in this naval base by the superior Japanese fleet, which launched a surprise attack in February 1904 and then prevented two break out attempts by the Russians.

Below: The Haruna*: originally a battlecruiser commissioned in 1915 and designed by the British naval engineer George Thurston. Later reclassified as a "fast battleship,"* Haruna *took part in many of the key actions of World War II, including the landings in Malaya and the battles of Midway, Philippine Sea, and Leyte Gulf. She was sunk at the Kure naval base by U.S. aircraft in 1945.*

July it invaded Indochina. The United States increased its financial aid to China to fight the Japanese. Then, with Britain and the Dutch East Indies, it put an embargo on imports to Japan. The restrictions were potentially catastrophic for Japan. The United States and the Dutch East Indies together provided Japan with some 80 percent of its oil.

Toward war

Japan's military planners saw only two options. They could accept the embargo, but would run out of oil by the end of 1942. Or they could go to war to seize territory in the Pacific and Indian Oceans. That would give them their own oil supplies. They chose the option that seemed to have the higher chance of success: war.

On October 18, Konoe resigned. He was replaced as prime minister by Hideki Tojo. War planning was already well advanced. Many in the Japanese leadership suspected that Japan could not hope to defeat the United States in a long war. Industrial power would prove decisive in a long conflict. Japan's best chance lay in a rapid victory.

In early November, Tojo proposed a number of diplomatic solutions to the United States. All of his proposals contained suggestions that were almost certain to prove unacceptable, however. They included the resumed sale of aviation fuel to Japan, the U.S. withdrawal from the Philippines, and the stopping of U.S. aid to China. All talks failed. On November 26, the U.S. secretary of state, Cordell Hull, issued his final ultimatums to Tojo. He demanded that the Japanese withdraw from China and Indochina and break their links with the Nazi regime.

The U.S. defiance, however, was now irrelevant. On that same day the Japanese war fleet sailed from positions north of Japan—its destination was Pearl Harbor.

Left: Akagi *(with flight deck) and the battleship* Nagato *at anchor. The* Nagato, *with its sister ship* Mutsu, *was the first in the world to be fitted with 16-in. guns. The two ships were also very fast, able to achieve 23 knots. They were certainly the most advanced battleships in the world during the 1920s.* Nagato *survived the war and was sunk as part of a nuclear test in 1946.*

Above: Admiral Togo, who comanded the Japanese fleet duing the Russo-Japanese war of 1904–1905 and masterminded the great victory of Tsushima.

Left: Kongo *undergoing refit in 1930. When launched* Kongo *was one of the first battleships to mount 14-in. guns.*

CHAPTER 2

PEARL HARBOR

December 7, 1941, stands in U.S. history as the "day of infamy" when Japan launched a surprise attack on the United States. The attack changed the course of World War II.

Previous pages:
Japanese fighter pilots ready their planes on the aircraft carrier Akagi, 230 miles (370km) north of Pearl Harbor. They headed to Hickam Field to attack U.S. airplanes on the ground and stop them from getting into the air.

The attack on Pearl Harbor had its roots in growing tension between the United States and Japan. Japan had territorial ambitions in the Pacific and China. It planned to create a "Greater East Asia Co-Prosperity Sphere." The United States had been involved in the Pacific since the late nineteenth century, when it took control of Hawaii and the Philippines. By 1940, the United States held naval bases across the Pacific.

The chief concern of the U.S. government was that a Japanese advance would threaten Allied, mainly British, possessions in Asia. That would weaken the British cause in World War II and aid Germany. Germany and Japan had signed a pact agreeing to come to each other's defense in the event of attack.

Roosevelt's strategy

The government of Franklin D. Roosevelt courted China as an ally. It thought the Chinese could help deter Japanese aggression. The United States provided the Nationalist government in China with trade credits and supplies. In May 1940, Roosevelt also sent the Pacific Fleet to Pearl Harbor on Hawaii in the Central Pacific. He aimed to deter Japanese aggression against British and Dutch possessions in Southeast Asia. Pearl Harbor became the largest U.S. outpost in the Pacific.

As tension grew between the United States and Japan, diplomatic movements continued. In February 1941, Japan sent a new ambassador to the United States, Kichisaburo Nomura. Nomura wanted peace, but later historians have questioned whether his government shared his commitment. In March, Nomura began talks with U.S. secretary of state Cordell Hull about China, which Japan had invaded in 1937. Hull demanded a Japanese withdrawal from China and the talks made little progress. Meanwhile, the Japanese continued their military build-up. Many Japanese politicians believed war was inevitable.

Imposing trade restrictions

In July 1941, Japan agreed with Vichy France that it could station 50,000 troops in French Indochina. (Vichy France was the part of France not occupied by Germany.) This put the Japanese Army and Navy within striking distance of Malaya, the Dutch East Indies, and the Philippines. They belonged to Britain, the Netherlands, and the United States respectively.

Roosevelt responded by freezing all Japanese assets in the United States. On August 1, he placed an embargo on oil exports to Japan, which depended on imported oil. Roosevelt also ordered General Douglas MacArthur to return to active duty, creating a new U.S. Army Forces Far East in the Philippines. Faced with this tough U.S. stance, the Japanese tried to initiate high-level talks. The United States insisted that Japan stop its expansionist activities and the talks broke down. Ultimately the oil embargo was one of the major factors that drove Japan to attack the United States in 1941.

> "Ultimately the oil embargo was one of the major factors that drove Japan to attack the United States in 1941"

Formulating a plan

When the embargo came into effect, the Japanese military had enough oil for only 18 months of combat. Prime minister Hideki Tojo considered options for a rapid campaign. He eventually decided on simultaneous attacks on the Philippines and Malaya, followed by an invasion of the Dutch East Indies to capture oil reserves.

The U.S. Navy remained a sticking point, however. Japan's war plans envisioned allowing the U.S. fleet to sail into the Central Pacific. There, the Imperial Japanese Navy would ambush and destroy it. Combined Fleet commander Admiral Isoroku Yamamoto thought the plan was bound to fail. In early 1941 he proposed the "Pearl Harbor Plan," for a surprise attack on Hawaii. Yamamoto had been educated at Harvard and knew the potential industrial strength of the United States. He thought that Japan would be unwise to instigate a war. If it did, however, he saw the Pearl Harbor plan as the only way forward.

Japanese sailors line the decks of an aircraft carrier as Mitsubishi A6M Reisen ("Zero") fighters take off for Pearl Harbor on December 7, 1941.

Yamamoto planned a strike on the U.S. base at Pearl Harbor on Oahu Island. It would cripple the U.S. Navy and delay any possible U.S. attack on the Japanese home islands by at least a year. The Japanese could then use the time to capture other U.S. bases and set up a defensive perimeter in the Pacific. The perimeter would allow them to exploit oil and rubber supplies in the "Southern Resource Area," centered on the Dutch East Indies. Tojo ordered the attack on December 4, 1941.

> "There was no reason for U.S. military leaders to suspect that Hawaii was the target"

The operation begins

On December 6, Roosevelt made a final appeal for peace to the emperor. By now, however, the plan to attack Pearl Harbor was underway. Six aircraft carriers and two battleships had sailed from the Japanese Kurile Islands on November 26. They were commanded by Admiral Chuichi Nagumo.

Maintaining radio silence to avoid detection, the task force sailed across the Pacific. It reached a position 230 miles (370 km) north of Pearl Harbor. Everything was ready.

Historians still debate how much the Allies knew about the coming attack. Some argue that the Allies most likely intercepted Japanese signals but failed to put them together. On November 30, U.S. intelligence decrypted a message from Tokyo to Berlin. It warned of imminent war: "There is extreme danger that war may suddenly break out between the Anglo-Saxon nations and Japan [and] this war may come quicker than anyone dreams." The message did not, however, contain any reason for U.S. military leaders to suspect that Hawaii was the target.

A final warning

Early on December 7, in Washington, D.C., U.S. Naval Intelligence intercepted a message from Japan telling Ambassador Nomura to break off negotiations with Cordell Hull. Army Intelligence decoded another message, sent at the same time. It ordered Nomura to submit his message to the State Department at precisely 13:00 hours (07:00 hours Hawaii time) and to destroy his code machines. Army Intelligence concluded that a U.S. base in East Asia would soon be attacked. It tried to reach Army chief of staff General George C. Marshall. Marshall was not reached until two hours later; he issued a warning to all U.S. forces to be on the alert. The message to Hawaii was delayed, however. The War Department had to send it by commercial telegraph because radio communications with the island were out of service.

The message only reached the U.S. Army commander in Hawaii, Walter C. Short, after the attack. Without a warning, the U.S. forces on Oahu were

ISOROKU YAMAMOTO

Admiral Isoroku Yamamoto was one of Japan's leading naval strategists. Considering the possibility of war with the United States, he remarked: "If in the face of such odds we decide to go to war—or rather are forced to do so by the trend of events—I can see little hope of success in any ordinary strategy." Yamamoto had traveled extensively in the United States, both as a student and later as a naval attaché. Understanding the industrial power of the United States, he went to war in 1941 with great trepidation. Yamamoto believed that the Pearl Harbor attack would buy Japan time to complete its conquests in Southeast Asia. He later set in motion the plans that led to the June 1942 Battle of Midway, where Japan lost naval supremacy in the Pacific. Yamamoto died when his aircraft was shot down in the Solomon Islands on April 18, 1943.

not ready to face an attack. They had not organized an effective defense. Several reports had identified an air raid as the most likely form of attack, probably in the early morning. Short and the U.S. Navy commander in Hawaii, Admiral Husband E. Kimmel, however, were more worried about the threat of sabotage. They had grouped ships together to make them easier to guard. For the same reason, the island's 400 aircraft were parked wing to wing on the airfields. This would make them an easy target for Japanese pilots. Both Short and Kimmel would lose their commands after the attack—unfairly, in the opinion of many historians.

Inside the anchorage at Pearl Harbor were 96 ships. They included the pride of the Pacific Fleet along Battleship Row: *Arizona*, *California*, *Iowa*, *Maryland*, *Nevada*, *Oklahoma*, *Tennessee*, *Utah*, *West Virginia*, and *Iowa*. The aircraft carriers *Lexington* and *Enterprise* were at sea, delivering aircraft to bases on Wake and Midway islands.

Incoming aircraft detected

The first part of the Japanese strike force took off from the carriers before dawn. It included 181 fighters, dive, and torpedo bombers. It was divided into four groups to head for the key targets: the anchorage at Pearl Harbor itself and the airfields at Kaneohe, Hickam, and Wheeler Field.

At 07:02 hours, a radar station in the north of Oahu detected 137 inbound aircraft and reported them to the Army Operations Center. The duty officer, Kermit Tyler, was a fighter pilot with no radar experience. He and a switchboard operator were the only people on duty. Tyler believed the aircraft to be B-17 bombers due from the mainland. He told the radar operator, "Don't worry

This aerial photograph of Pearl Harbor, taken during the attack of December 7, 1941, shows the inviting target the assembled U.S. warships offered Japanese pilots.

21

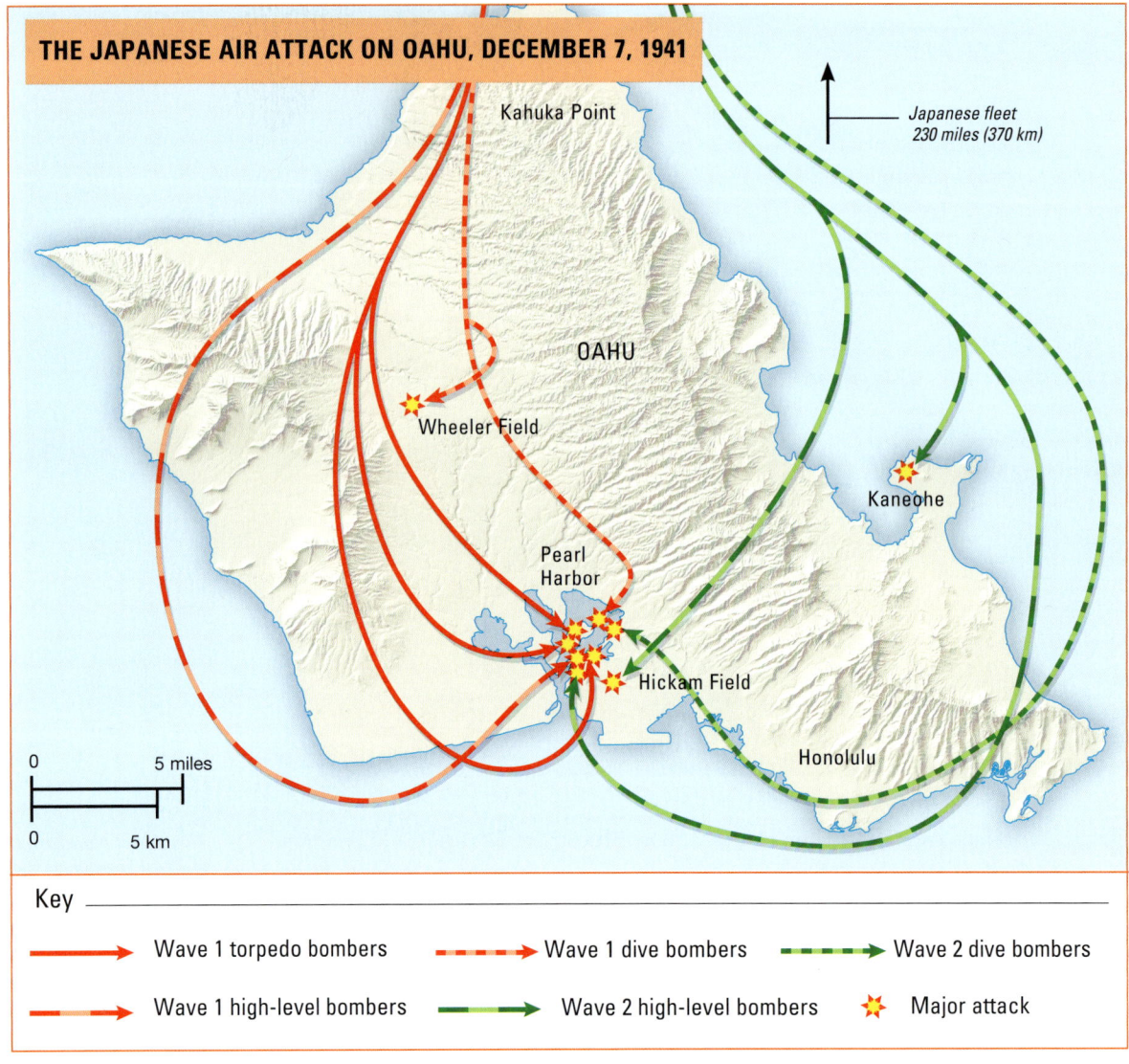

THE JAPANESE AIR ATTACK ON OAHU, DECEMBER 7, 1941

Kahuka Point

Japanese fleet 230 miles (370 km)

OAHU

Wheeler Field

Kaneohe

Pearl Harbor

Hickam Field

Honolulu

0   5 miles

0   5 km

Key

→ Wave 1 torpedo bombers   ▸▸▸ Wave 1 dive bombers   ▸▸▸ Wave 2 dive bombers

→ Wave 1 high-level bombers   ▸▸▸ Wave 2 high-level bombers   ✸ Major attack

The paths taken by the two arms of the Japanese attack targeted the island's airfields as well as the harbor itself.

about it." The radar station then shut down for the day as scheduled.

Tora! Tora! Tora!

As Japanese aircraft approached Oahu, the USS *Ward*, a destroyer on routine patrol, attacked a midget submarine at the entrance to Pearl Harbor. The craft was one of five intended to torpedo ships once the air attack had started. News of the incident reached Kimmel and his Pacific Fleet staff. They requested confirmation of the report. Commander Mitsuo Fuchida led the strike force above Oahu. At 07:53 hours,

he radioed back to the fleet the code words *"Tora! Tora! Tora!"* ("Tiger! Tiger! Tiger!"). The message meant that the Japanese had achieved complete surprise. Fuchida could not believe what he saw. He later recalled: "I have seen our own warships assembled for review before the emperor, but I have never seen ships, even in the deepest peace, anchored at a distance less than 500 to 1000 yards from each other... The picture down there was hard to comprehend."

The attack began as soldiers, sailors, and Marines went about their Sunday-morning routines. Dive bombers and fighters hit the air bases. The torpedo bombers headed for the fleet. They carried weapons specially redesigned for the shallow anchorage.

On Battleship Row, the *Arizona*, *California*, and *Oklahoma* suffered several direct hits, caught fire, and sank. More than 1,100 of the *Arizona*'s 1,500 crew were killed. Many were trapped below decks and drowned. The *West Virginia*, meanwhile, was holed and took on a huge amount of water. It tipped severely to one side. The ship's captain ordered the flooding of the other side of the ship, to bring it back upright. The maneuver allowed many of the crew to escape before the vessel eventually sank.

The air bases suffered similar destruction. Squadrons of flying boats at the Kaneohe Bay naval air base were destroyed on the ground. The same happened to fighters at Hickam, Wheeler, and Bellows fields.

The flight of B-17 Flying Fortresses

Eyewitness Report:

" It was just like the newsreels of Europe, only worse. We saw a bunch of soldiers come running full tilt toward us from the barracks and just then a whole line of bombs fell behind them, knocking them all to the ground. A bunch of soldiers had come into our garage to hide. They were entirely taken by surprise and most of them didn't even have a gun or anything. One of them asked for a drink of water. He had just been so close to where a bomb fell that he had been showered with debris. "

Ginger, U.S. schoolgirl, Hawaii, 1941

Smoke billows from the USS West Virginia *after the Japanese attack. The ship sank, but was later salvaged. The* Tennessee, *beyond the* West Virginia, *was less seriously damaged; its crew fought to control fires on nearby ships.*

Rescuers stand on the upturned hull of the USS Oklahoma *in the aftermath of the Japanese attack. A total of 429 sailors died when the battleship capsized. The USS* Maryland, *in the background, was also damaged, but not severely.*

due from the mainland arrived at the height of the attack. They had been stripped of weapons and ammunition for the long flight to Hawaii and had no defenses. However, the B-17s survived to land successfully at Hickam Field.

Mass destruction

The reaction of the U.S. forces to the attack was heroic but ineffective. The commander of the battleship *Nevada* got the ship underway as the attack began. It took only 45 minutes instead of the usual two hours. *Nevada* fired its antiaircraft guns as it steamed down the channel. On the *West Virginia*, African American cook Doris "Dorie" Miller manned an anti-aircraft gun, for which he had no training. He won the Navy Cross for his brave action. The attack ended at 08:30 hours. The island's defenders took the chance to improve

their readiness. When a second wave of 170 planes arrived at 09:00 hours, antiaircraft crews downed 20 of them. Many more got through, however, damaging ships in dry dock.

A devastating raid

When the attackers departed at 10:00 hours, they left a scene of destruction. Five battleships were sunk or sinking. Eight more ships were damaged. Some 320 airplanes had been destroyed or damaged and the runways of the air bases were cratered and littered with wreckage. Black smoke hung over the harbor and the airfields. There were 2,335 men killed and more than 1,000 wounded. Burning oil slicks covered the harbor. They hampered recovery crews who raced to rescue men trapped underwater. Japanese losses, meanwhile,

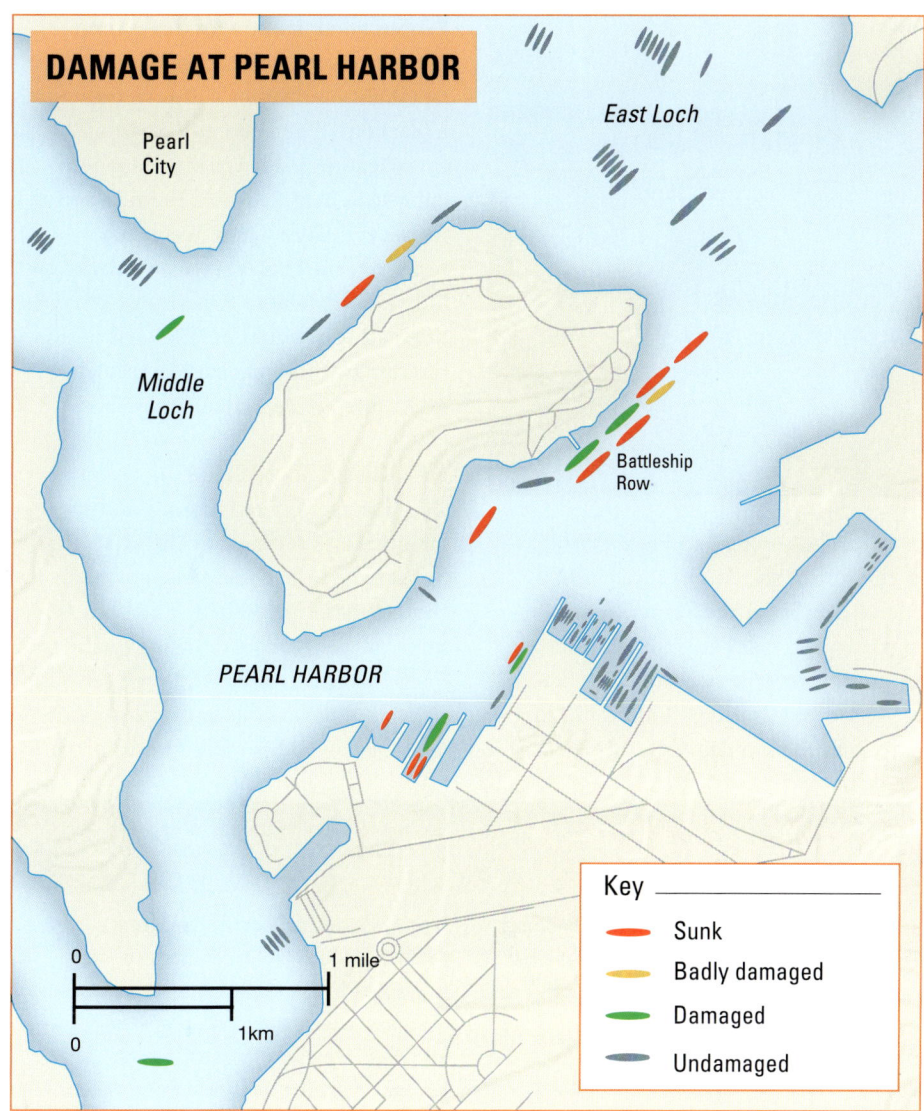

DAMAGE AT PEARL HARBOR

Pearl City

East Loch

Middle Loch

Battleship Row

PEARL HARBOR

0   1 mile

0   1km

Key

■ Sunk

■ Badly damaged

■ Damaged

■ Undamaged

This diagram shows where U.S. vessels were sunk or damaged. Most of the five battleships lost were sunk in the first wave of the attack.

were between 30 and 60 aircraft, the five midget submarines, and fewer than 100 men.

December 7, 1941

It was early afternoon on the U.S. East Coast when word of the attack began to come in. Nomura had been unable to deliver his message at 13:00 hours, as his government had instructed. He arrived at the State Department only after the attack had begun. Roosevelt met with his military advisers. In the next 24 hours, they received reports of attacks on other U.S. and Allied bases in

the Pacific: Guam, Wake Island, Hong Kong, and Singapore.

Roosevelt drafted a request for a declaration of war against Japan. He delivered the request in a six-minute address to Congress at noon on December 8: "Yesterday, December 7, 1941, a date which will live in infamy, the United States of America was suddenly and deliberately attacked by naval and air forces of the Empire of Japan." The Senate voted unanimously to declare war; in the House of Representatives, only Senator Jeannette Rankin of Montana voted against going

On December 8, 1941, President Roosevelt asked Congress for a declaration of war against Japan. The president's "Infamy" speech was broadcast around the world. Within half an hour, the United States was at war.

On Wake Island, U.S. aircraft lie destroyed after the Japanese raid of 1941. Although U.S. troops fought off the first attacks, they were eventually forced to surrender.

People filled the streets. They fired guns at passing aircraft and smashed car headlights and street lamps to create a blackout. The Federal Bureau of Investigation (FBI) arrested Japanese American men and held them in prison for several days. There were also a series of unprovoked civilian attacks on individual Japanese Americans, or Nisei. Such attacks would be followed within months by the organized large-scale internment of Japanese Americans.

A change of tactics

The damage to Pearl Harbor and its facilities was severe, but the attack had not affected the Pacific Fleet as badly as the Japanese had hoped. The bombs hit none of the massive refueling facilities at Pearl Harbor. Neither did they seriously damage its dry docks and repair yards. The fleet would be able to use the yards

to war. The reaction to Pearl Harbor in the rest of the country was initially one of panic. On the West Coast, in particular, many people expected an imminent Japanese attack. In San Francisco, the National Guard began patrolling the Golden Gate Bridge.

WAKE ISLAND

Wake Island was a small U.S. Navy outpost in the Western Pacific. The island was a coral atoll with a 5,000-foot (1.5km) airstrip. It was defended by 450 men led by Major J.P.S. Devereux and a Marine fighter squadron. Japanese bombers struck Wake on December 8, 1941.

They destroyed most of the fighter planes, although the Japanese also lost many aircraft to coastal guns. When the Japanese tried to land on December 11, U.S. gun crews damaged or sank several ships. The Japanese troop convoy turned back. News of the successful defense elated the U.S. public.

The Japanese continued with daily bombings, however, while the arrival of a U.S. relief force was delayed. When the Japanese landing force returned on December 23, the defenders, outnumbered five to one, surrendered.

Control of Wake Island was strategically vital to the Japanese. It allowed them to set up a secure line of communication across the Central Pacific. This isolated the Philippines and exposed Douglas MacArthur's forces there to attack.

throughout the war to repair damaged ships. More significantly, perhaps, the U.S. aircraft carriers had escaped the attack. That meant that the Pacific Fleet still had the ability to carry out long-range operations. In effect, the attack forced the U.S. Navy to modernize its tactics. It could not depend on the big guns of battleships. The dominant weapon in naval combat for the rest of the war would be carrier-borne aircraft. The "flattops" and their pilots would stop the Japanese advance in the Coral Sea and win decisive victories at Midway, the Philippine Sea, and Leyte Gulf later in the war.

The United States joins the war

The most important legacies of the Pearl Harbor attack were strategic and emotional. Anger over the attack finally ensured that Americans abandoned their isolationism. They backed the country's entry into the war, two years after fighting had broken out in Europe. Jeannette Rankin's vote against war—she had taken a similar stand before the United States entered World War I—this time cost her her political career. "Remember Pearl Harbor!" became a rallying cry, spurring industrial production and military efforts.

On December 11, meanwhile, Adolf Hitler declared war on the United States. Although Germany and Japan were members of the Tripartite Pact, there was no real reason Hitler had to declare war at this stage. His reasons for doing so remain uncertain. He probably believed that war with the United States was inevitable at some time. He was said to be elated when news came through of Pearl Harbor, because he saw the Japanese as strong allies.

Hitler's decision meant that Roosevelt was able to enter the

WHAT DID ROOSEVELT KNOW?

The greatest controversy surrounding Pearl Harbor concerns how much Franklin D. Roosevelt knew of Japanese plans before the attack. Several historians have suggested that Roosevelt ignored warnings about the attack from U.S. intelligence. They say he wanted an excuse to take the United States into the war.

One main controversy concerns the difference between Roosevelt having a sense that an attack might be imminent, which he may have had, and his having specific knowledge that Pearl Harbor was the target and not warning the military there, which is very unlikely. There were many rumors in Washington, D.C., that war was coming. The most likely explanation is that the president and his advisers did expect an attack, but that they believed it would be against British and Dutch colonies in East and Southeast Asia, rather than against the U.S. Pacific Fleet.

war in Europe without encountering any domestic opposition. The benefit to the rest of the Allies of the full entry of the United States into the war was obvious. The "arsenal of democracy" brought the Allies new supplies of resources, industrial strength, vast reserves of personnel, and stronger political leadership. In a well-known—but probably inaccurate—story, British prime minister Winston Churchill was woken up to learn the news of the attack at Pearl Harbor. He remarked: "Well, we've won then!" In a few hours, the attack had begun the process of turning the United States into the leader of the Allied coalition.

The Pearl Harbor attack provoked a backlash against Japanese Americans, such as this girl waiting to be sent to an internment camp in 1942.

CHAPTER 3
THE DEFEAT OF THE BRITISH AND DUTCH

The attack on Pearl Harbor was just the start of Japan's campaign of conquest in the Pacific. Its commanders launched a rapid onslaught against Allied forces to secure a series of conquests in the region.

Previous pages:
Japanese troops
advance through a
rubber plantation
in Malaya in 1942.
Malaya was a major
producer of rubber,
a material crucial to
Japan's industrial
needs.

British troops erect
barbed-wire defenses
along Hong Kong's
rocky shore.

Many Japanese officers understood that there were great risks in a long war against the United States and Britain. Admiral Isoroku Yamamoto was commander of the Combined Fleet. He thought that the Japanese might have the advantage for six months in the Pacific. Then the industrial power of the United States would come to bear on the conflict.

The Japanese developed a short-term strategy to achieve their long-term goals. They aimed to acquire territories that were rich in resources or strategic-ally important. Their targets included the Dutch East Indies (now Indonesia) and the British colonies of Malaya, Singapore, Hong Kong, and Burma, as well as the U.S.-ruled Philippines. They also aimed to create a line of defenses to protect the captured territory and the Japanese home islands.

The defensive perimeter was to stretch from the Kurile Islands south to Rabaul on New Britain. It would pass through Wake Island, the Marianas, the Carolinas, the Marshalls, and the Gilberts. From Rabaul, it would extend west to northwestern New Guinea, taking in the East Indies, Malaya, Thailand, and Burma.

The Japanese thought that the Allies would wear themselves out attacking this perimeter. They would eventually negotiate peace and leave Japan in possession of its conquests. The plan depended on speed. For six months after the attack on Pearl Harbor on December 7, 1941, the Japanese forces swept all before them.

The first defeats

On December 8 (the same day as the Pearl Harbor attack, but on the other side of the international date line), Japan invaded Thailand and northern Malaya. It also attacked Hong Kong. Japanese infantry occupied some smaller islands in the Philippines. Aircraft launched attacks on the U.S. garrison on Wake Island, midway between the Philippines and Hawaii. By December 13, the Japanese had driven British defenders from the New Territories on the Chinese mainland to the island of Hong Kong. Overnight on December 18/19, the Japanese landed on the island. After hard fighting, the British surrendered on Christmas Day.

Strenuous defense

On Wake Island, meanwhile, the 450 U.S. Marines had put up a strong defense. When the Japanese sent a landing fleet to the island on December 11, U.S. aircraft and artillery sank two destroyers and a transport ship. They forced the fleet to withdraw. Under heavy bombardment, the Wake Island garrison held out until December 23, when the Japanese put troops ashore.

By Christmas, Japanese forces had taken control of other Pacific territory, such as the Gilbert Islands. On the Asian mainland, meanwhile, they were about to inflict on the British one of the worst defeats in their military history.

Fighting the British

The Japanese attack began on the night of December 7/8 with two amphibious landings. One division landed in Thailand, just north of the border with Malaya. Another landed on Malaya's northeastern coast. The Japanese forces had about 60,000 men in total. They advanced in two columns. One headed down the east of the country, the other down the west.

Facing the advance was a force of British and Commonwealth troops led by Lieutenant-General Arthur Percival. With 88,000 men, Percival had more troops than the Japanese, but the Japanese were better armed. They also had 459 modern aircraft and 80 tanks. The British had no armor and only

Japanese soldiers advance along a jungle road with their supplies loaded onto bicycles. The use of bicycles greatly increased the mobility and speed of the Japanese advance in Southeast Asia.

British seamen scramble over the side of the torpedoed HMS Prince of Wales *before the ship finally sinks on December 9, 1941.*

158 aircraft, many of which were old. The Japanese troops were trained in jungle warfare and included many combat veterans. By contrast the Allied soldiers had no special training. Believing the jungle to be impenetrable, for example, the British set up road blocks to stop the Japanese. The Japanese simply moved off the roads and advanced through the vegetation.

Thailand and Malaya

North of the Malayan border, Japan secured control of Thailand, which surrendered on December 9. In Malaya, meanwhile, Japanese troops made swift

THE SINKING OF THE PRINCE OF WALES AND REPULSE

In October 1941, Britain sent a force of warships to protect the waters around Malaya and Singapore in the event of a war with Japan. British prime minister Winston Churchill sent the brand-new battleship HMS *Prince of Wales*, the battle cruiser HMS *Repulse*, and four destroyers. The force was named "Force Z." It was commanded by Vice-Admiral Sir Tom Phillips. It arrived at Singapore on December 2. Only six days later, the Japanese invaded Malaya.

Phillips sailed his ships up the Malaya coast. He aimed to stop the Japanese from making amphibious landings to the north. It was a high-risk strategy: Force Z would have no air cover against Japanese attack aircraft and would be outnumbered by Japanese vessels.

On December 9, Force Z was spotted by Japanese aircraft. Phillips decided that the risks were too great and turned his fleet back. It was too late, however. A Japanese force of 52 torpedo planes and 34 bombers soon attacked. Torpedoes struck both the *Prince of Wales* and the *Repulse*; within hours, both had sunk. The losses were a huge blow to the pride of the British Royal Navy, for decades the world's most powerful navy. Churchill later said: "In all the war, I never received a more direct shock."

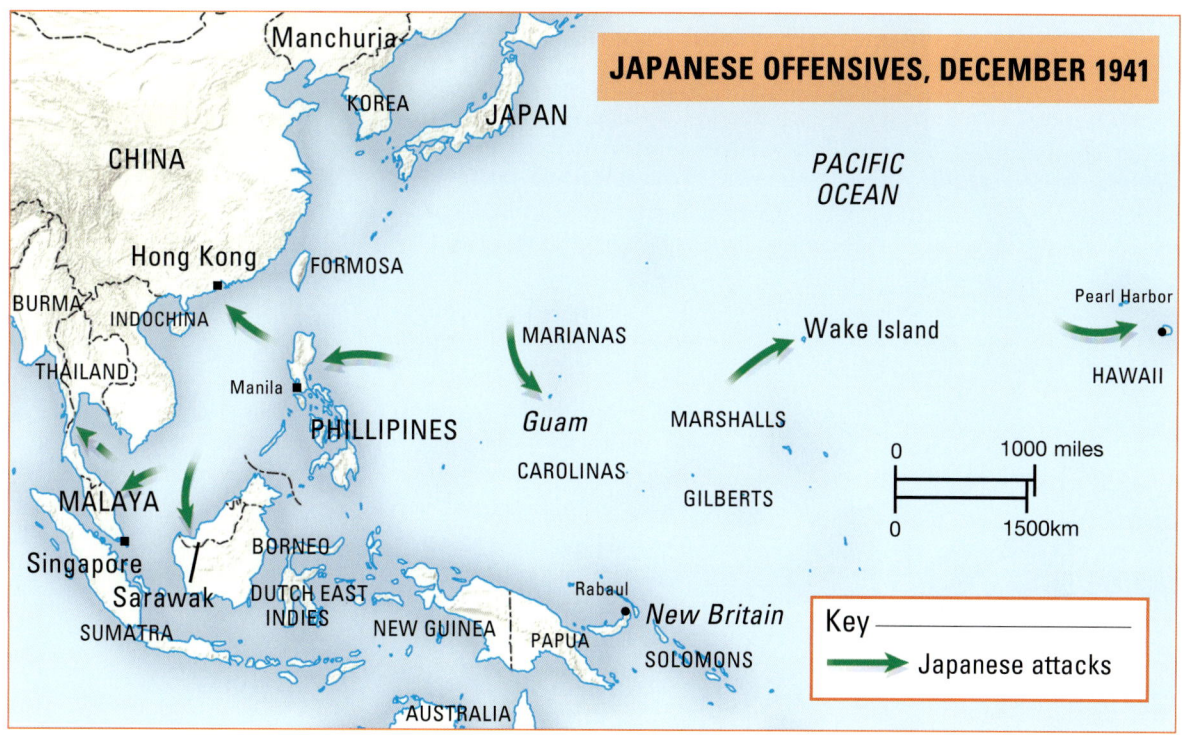

JAPANESE OFFENSIVES, DECEMBER 1941

Key —————
→ Japanese attacks

progress down the mainland. They gained control of oil fields in the north of the country. The Japanese were highly mobile. They covered ground quickly, even in thick jungle. They made a series of amphibious "jumps" along the coast to get behind the British frontline. The destruction of a powerful Royal Navy force by the Japanese on December 9 meant that the British could not oppose these landings.

The Japanese took the town of Jitra on December 12. They swept south to break a line of Allied defenses along the Slim River. The British retreated south toward the capital, Kuala Lumpur, where Percival had his headquarters. Between January 1 and 10, 1942, more Japanese amphibious landings outflanked the Allied defensive line near the town of Kampar. Kampar fell on January 3 and the Japanese came to within 20 miles (32km) of Kuala Lumpur. The British abandoned the capital, which fell on January 11.

Japan had conquered two-thirds of Malaya, a remarkable achievement. The rapid advance had resulted in the decimation of British air units. Around 100 British aircraft were lost in the first week. It had also brought the Japanese control of captured airfields. They extended their superior air cover south toward the end of the Malay peninsula and Singapore.

Local Allied resistance briefly helped to raise morale among the retreating Allies. It did little to slow the pace of the Japanese advance, however. The Allies were driven back toward Johor, the southern tip of Malaya.

Retreat to Singapore

Defeat in mainland Malaya was now a virtual certainty. Allied forces had only one place to retreat to: Singapore, just off the southern tip of the peninsula. Although only 266 square miles (683 sq km), the island was one of Britain's most important colonies in East Asia. It

Japan launched a series of attacks across Southeast Asia in 1941 to seize strategic bases and economic resources.

33

YAMASHITA, THE TIGER OF MALAYA

General Tomoyuki Yamashita became known as "the Tiger of Malaya" after his eight-week victory over Allied forces there. He began his military career in 1906 as an infantry officer. His intelligence and resolve saw him rise through the ranks of the military and political establishment in Japan. Yamashita led units in Korea and Manchuria before being appointed commander of the Twenty-Fifth Army in November 1941. After his victory in Malaya in January 1942, he was promoted to full general.

Prime Minister Hideki Tojo—a long-standing political rival—then posted him to Manchuria in northern China, far from the main conflict. After Tojo resigned in July 1944, Yamashita led the defense of the Philippines. He surrendered on September 2, 1945.

After the war, Yamashita was found guilty of war crimes committed by Navy troops in Manila, the Philippine capital. He was hanged on February 23, 1946. It is now widely accepted that he knew nothing about the atrocities.

Tomoyuki Yamashita became a national hero in Japan after his victory over Allied troops in Malaya.

had become a British territory in 1824 and had grown into a thriving commercial and military port. The island gave Britain command of vital sea routes to the Dutch East Indies, India, and Australia.

Singapore's importance was reflected in the batteries of naval guns that protected it. However, the guns were useless to repel the Japanese. They were set up to face a seaward attack. The Japanese assault came from mainland Malaya. More crucially, the guns and their ammunition were designed for firing at ships over long distances, not for anti-personnel use.

The British defense of Malaya ended on January 31, 1942. The last British troops crossed the Johor Strait to Singapore. The defeat had cost the British 4,000 dead and 21,000 prisoners, against Japanese losses of 2,000 dead and 3,000 wounded.

Percival allocated his men to defensive positions on Singapore. It seemed as if the British might now have the advantage.

Defending Singapore

Percival had received reinforcements. At the beginning of February, his total troop numbers were around 85,000. The Japanese commander, Tomoyuki Yamashita, had only 35,000 troops, although he had greater air and armor resources. Yet British commanders were concerned about defending Singapore. Percival was warned about its defensive weaknesses by his superior, General Sir Archibald Wavell, the Allied Supreme Commander in East Asia. Wavell was concerned about the northwest of the island. Understrength Australian battalions were guarding a long stretch of coastline there. Percival made a fatal error in his defensive plans, however.

Eyewitness Report:

" Dodging bombs and shells, I eventually approached the city of Singapore. Hundreds of unburied dead almost blocked the streets and the smell of putrefying flesh mingling with the bombed sewerage was appalling. A huge black pall of smoke from the blazing oil tanks on Pulau Bukum and the Naval Base hung over the city and the rain drops were turning black as they reached the ground. Fires blazed everywhere, wrecked cars littered the streets with the dead, Jap planes bombed at will and armed soldiers were wandering about bewildered; what unbelievable chaos. "

**R.G. Curry, lieutenant commander,
British Royal Navy
Singapore City, February 12, 1942**

He concentrated his forces in order to defend naval and air installations on the east of the island. When the Japanese attacked, they came from the west.

Assault on Singapore

The Japanese assault on Singapore began on the night of February 8/9. Infantry of the Japanese 5th and 18th Divisions crossed the Johor Strait. They attacked the Australians in the northwest, as Wavell had feared. There was vicious fighting, often at close quarters. The Australians fought back the first two Japanese landing forces. However, a third force secured a beachhead and began to push the Allies inland.

The next night, troops of the Japanese Imperial Guards Division crossed the strait and attacked in the northwest. The first attacks were stopped on the beaches. A confused order from a local commander then led the Allied defenders to withdraw. They fell back to the Jurong Line, a defensive line across the center of the island. The mistake allowed Japanese troops to get ashore without resistance. They began to overwhelm the island.

The fall of Singapore

In Singapore City itself, civilians panicked under constant bombing and shelling. The Jurong Line was the last hope for an effective defense, but the Japanese broke through on February 11. They captured the island's main water reservoirs the next day. This gave them a crucial advantage. If they cut off water supplies, dehydration might cause many deaths.

A British infantryman surrenders during the Japanese advance in Malaya.

On February 15, Percival met his senior officers. Unknown to them, Yamashita's forces had been weakened by the weeks of fighting. They possibly would not have had the strength to overwhelm the island's defenders had they put up a prolonged fight. After pessimistic reports at the commanders' conference, however, Percival decided to surrender. About 130,000 British, Commonwealth, and Malay soldiers were taken prisoner. They represented a large proportion of British military strength in Asia.

Yamashita had suffered around 5,000 casualties. The victory was a spectacular achievement for the Japanese and an unmitigated disaster for the Allies.

Japanese troops celebrate their rapid conquest of Malaya with a captured railroad locomotive.

The Dutch East Indies

The Japanese had made significant landings in mid-December 1941 in Sarawak on Borneo, one of the largest islands of the Dutch East Indies. Their main offensive began in January 1942. It involved three Japanese forces. Western Force would attack Sumatra, Java, and British North Borneo. Eastern Force would strike at the islands of Celebes and Amboina before advancing into the far south of the Dutch East Indies. Central Force aimed to take Borneo.

The offensive began on January 10, 1942. Initial operations went smoothly, despite some localized resistance. By the end of January, Japan had conquered the coastlines of almost all of the central and

eastern islands. A landing at Balikpapan on January 24 brought most of Borneo's oil fields under Japanese control.

Futile resistance

In February the Japanese widened their operations. On February 14, Western Force began its attacks on Sumatra. It made extensive parachute landings around Palembang. British and Commonwealth defenders met the paratroopers with heavy anti-aircraft fire. The next day, the Allies launch-ed an air attack against a Japanese amphibious landing. It sank one ship, killing dozens of men. The Allies wasted their successes, however, by making a premature withdrawal.

Java and the Java Sea

By the end of February, much of central and southern Sumatra was in Japanese hands. On March 1, Japanese forces made major landings along the northern coast of Java.

The decisive moment of the conquest of the Dutch East Indies was one of the largest naval battles since World War I: the Battle of the Java Sea. On February 27, Rear Admiral Doorman sent five cruisers and nine destroyers to intercept a Japanese invasion force off Java. Protecting the Japanese force were 4 cruisers and 14 destroyers.

The battle began in the late afternoon. Although the forces were relatively evenly matched, the Japanese were skilled at fighting at night. They also had stocks of fast, long-range torpedos. The British cruiser HMS *Exeter* was hit by a Japanese shell, but remained afloat. Soon after, the Dutch destroyer *Kortenar* was hit by a torpedo. It blew up before sinking. The destroyer HMS *Electra* was hit by shells and sank.

By about 18:30 hours, Doorman's force was greatly reduced. Four U.S. destroyers had to leave the combat area to refuel. Nevertheless, the rear admiral took his remaining vessels to hunt out

The Dutch flagship De Ruyter *was sunk in the Battle of the Java Sea. The action was disastrous for the Allied defense of the Dutch East Indies.*

37

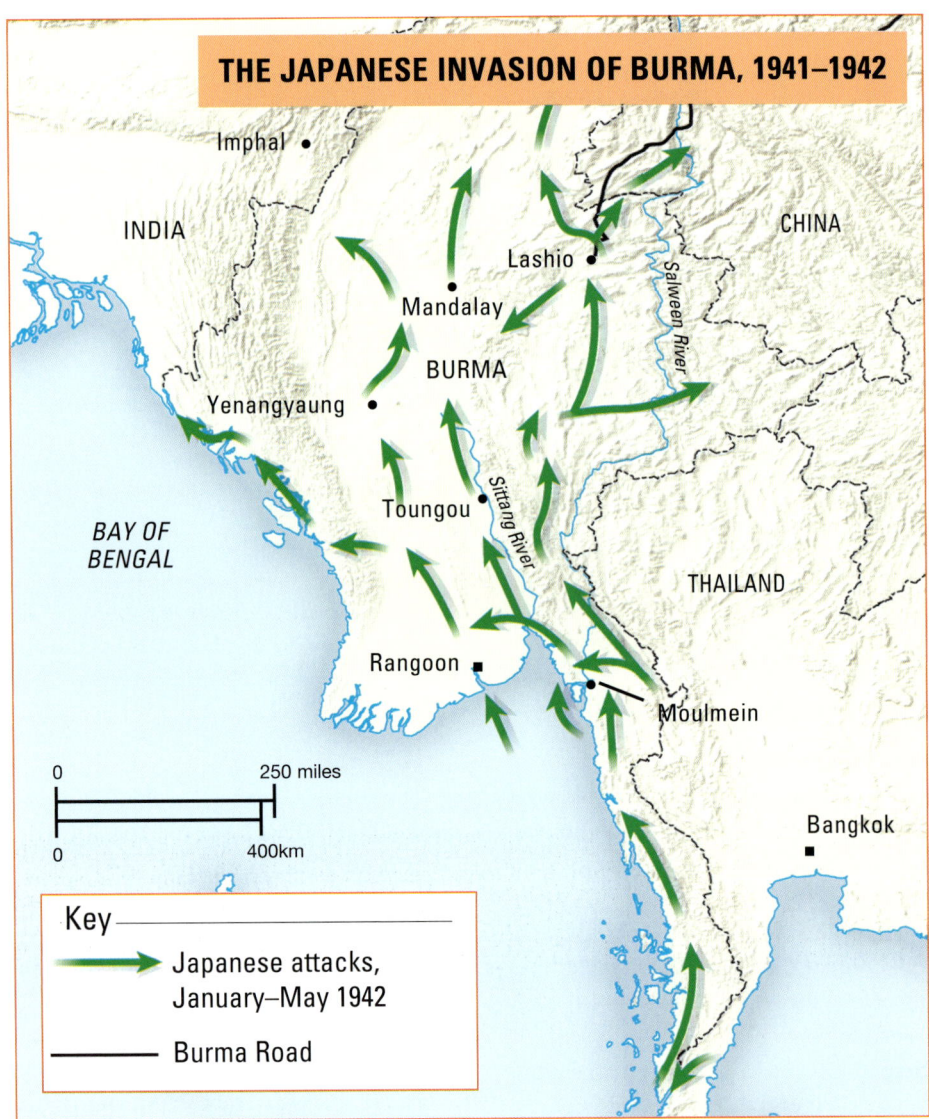

THE JAPANESE INVASION OF BURMA, 1941–1942

Key

→ Japanese attacks, January–May 1942

— Burma Road

The rapid Japanese advances through Burma drove the British back into India and the Chinese back into China.

the Japanese force in the darkness. It was a disastrous decision. HMS *Jupiter* struck a mine and blew up. When the Allies found the Japanese vessels, torpedo attacks sank the *De Ruyter* and the *Java*. Doorman died in the attack on *De Ruyter*. Five more Allied ships were sunk in the next two days. The disaster marked the virtual end of resistance to Japan's conquest of the Dutch East Indies. All the islands had surrendered by March 8.

In mainland Southeast Asia, the Japanese had invaded Burma in December 1941. They wanted to control the British colony to protect the Japanese invasion of Malaya.

Plans in Burma

The Japanese in Burma would be able to stop British troops advancing from British India to the west. Burma would also provide a potential starting place for an invasion of India itself.

Burma was defended by about 27,000 troops, but many of them were of poor quality. The far north of the country was protected by the Chinese. Two Chinese divisions were led by the U.S. commander "Vinegar" Joe Stilwell. Allied air support was virtually non-existent. Nevertheless, the Allies expected the Japanese to make slow progress. Burma had mountainous jungles divided by rivers that would provide good defensive positions.

The Burma campaign

In December 1941, Japanese forces invaded the far south of Burma from Thailand. They were followed on January 20, 1942, by the main invasion force. This was the Japanese Fifteenth Army. It comprised about 35,000 men led by General Shojira Iida. The Japanese overran the town of Kawkareik. They pushed north toward the Burmese capital, Rangoon, which lay in the southern half of the country. By January

26, the Japanese had reached Moulmein. British resistance in the town collapsed on January 30.

Major-General John Smyth commanded the 17th Indian Division. He argued that all Allied troops should pull back to the Sittang River. The river would form a natural defense to break up the assault. The British high command hesitated. They did not agree to the plan until February 19. By then the Japanese had inflicted heavy losses on the British defenders around the Salween and Bilin rivers.

The Allied retreat from Burma

When the Allied fallback did begin, both sides raced to reach the main bridge across the Sittang in the town of the same name. After hand-to-hand fighting around the river, the Allies

Indian troops in the British Army advance through a plantation during the campaign in Malaya.

THE FALL OF SINGAPORE

The fall of Singapore was a huge shock to the British. The island had been thought impregnable but the Japanese Army took it easily.

Below: A symbol of the changing world order as Japanese troops march past the General Post Office in Singapore.

The island of Singapore occupied a vital position at the tip of the Malay peninsula and was a potent symbol of Britain's imperial might. Singapore City, a major port, was protected by large numbers of heavy guns, but these were all sited to resist an attack from the sea. The Japanese had no intention of attacking into a hail of heavy artillery fire. They moved down the Malay peninsula and the first attacks on the fortress city came from the air.

The British had not only placed defensive armament in what turned out to be the wrong place; they had also seriously underestimated the potential of the Japanese armed forces. Casual racist attitudes permeated British views of their foe. The standard cartoon of a Japanese character always portrayed him with buck teeth and thick glasses and it was widely believed, therefore, that Japanese pilots had poor eyesight

and that their air force was bound to be inferior to British aviation. Quite the opposite was the case and the Japanese air force was a major factor in their victory.

The news of the fall of Singapore astonished politicians in London. The immediate reaction was that its fall was due to the "guns pointing the wrong way." However, the truth was even more shocking. The British forces were simply not able to compete with the mobile, highly motivated Japanese troops of General Yamashita. The British, Empire and Commonwealth troops that surrendered in Singapore outnumbered their foe by about two to one. But they had been penned up and rendered impotent because they could not match the skills that the soldiers of the Rising Sun showed as they moved south through Malaya.

managed to blow up the bridge before the Japanese could cross. The action also left thousands of Allies stranded on the wrong side of the river, however. The 17th Indian Division lost 5,000 men killed or captured.

Lieutenant-General Thomas Hutton, in charge of Burma, ordered that Rangoon be abandoned. Wavell disagreed. He replaced Hutton with Lieutenant-General Sir Harold Alexander. Alexander agreed with Hutton, however. "Burcorps," as the British and Allied forces were known, continued their retreat. Rangoon fell to the Japanese on March 8.

Reinforcements arrived from the Chinese Fifth and Sixth Armies, but they were defeated at Toungou on March 30. On May 1, the Japanese took Mandalay. The city was nearly 1,000 miles (1,600km) north of where the campaign had begun. Alexander realized that defending Burma was impossible. On April 25, he ordered Burcorps to retreat to India. The remaining Chinese forces would head back to their homeland.

The Allied retreat to India

The retreat to India was one of the longest in British military history: over 600 miles (1,000km) in nine weeks. The first Allied units entered India on May 19. They were weakened by aerial attack, ground combat, and disease. Burcorps had lost a total of 13,000 men in Burma, compared to 5,000 Japanese casualties. In only six months the Japanese had won a stunning series of victories in Southeast Asia. The Dutch and British colonial empires had collapsed. In air, sea, and land warfare the Imperial Japanese forces had proved manifestly superior to their enemies.

Above: Japanese infantry mounted on bicycles cross a bridge on their way south through Malaya. A key battle in the invasion of Malaya was that at Muar, 100 miles (160km) north of Singapore itself. A major defensive position was smashed by the Japanese 5th and 8th Infantry Divisions and the British lost 3,700 men killed, wounded, or captured.

Above: The surrender of Singapore was accompanied by atrocities committed by Japanese troops. The day before the surrender (which took place on February 15) the Japanese killed 150 staff and patients at the Queen Alexandra military hospital. The 62,000 Allied personnel who went into captivity suffered severely at the hands of their captors, through open brutality, overwork, and neglect.

Left: A column of Japanese Type 95 light tanks in Malaya. These were light vehicles, unsuited to combat with standard Allied tanks, but their mobility was what counted in December 1941/January 1942 as they plunged forward, going round strongpoints and catching out the British infantry on the Malay peninsula.

Right: Japanese infantry in action in China. The war in China, which had begun in 1937, had given the Japanese Army valuable combat experience that the West had ignored as a factor.

41

CHAPTER 4
THE FALL OF THE PHILIPPINES

The capture of the Philippines was a crucial part of Japan's strategy to secure an empire in the Southwest Pacific and to remove U.S. power from the region. Hours after the raid on Pearl Harbor, Japan attacked the islands.

Previous pages:
Japanese troops land on the island of Corregidor on May 6, 1942. Corregidor, the last U.S. stronghold in the Philippines, fell to the Japanese later in the day.

The Philippines are a group of about 7,000 islands in the Pacific. They were of great strategic importance because they lay between Japan on the one hand and Southeast Asia and the islands of the Dutch East Indies (Indonesia) on the other. Those territories were rich in resources that the Japanese needed, such as oil. With the region under its control, Japan could then move southeast to secure bases on New Guinea and the Solomon Islands. Japanese possession of the Solomons would limit communications between Australia and the United States. That would hamper Allied operations in the Southwest Pacific.

The Philippines became a U.S. colony in 1898, at the end of the Spanish–American War. The U.S. Navy began to use Manila Bay. Located off Luzon, the largest and most northerly of the Philippine islands, the bay was one of the finest fleet anchorages in Asia.

By the mid-1930s, however, the U.S. Navy was short of funds. There were few ships at the naval base. The United States had also stopped building fortifications in the Philippines under the 1922 Washington Naval Treaty. The treaty was intended to reduce tensions in the Pacific. As a result, only the islands near the entrance to Manila Bay were well protected.

In any case, the U.S. government planned to withdraw from the Philippines. It could not defend a colony 3,000 miles (5,000km) from the nearest U.S. base on Hawaii. It gave the Filipinos some self-government in 1935 and promised full independence in 1946. In the meantime, defense of the islands would be handed over gradually to the Philippine government, despite its limited resources.

Growing Japanese power

Meanwhile Japanese power grew, isolating the Philippines. To the north Japan had colonized Formosa (Taiwan). To the east, it had taken over the Palau, Caroline, and Marshall islands as part of the Versailles Treaty of 1919. Japan's possessions east of the Philippines formed a chain broken only by two U.S.-controlled islands: Guam and Wake. In 1939 Japan struck west, across the South China Sea. Japanese troops occupied the island of Hainan in January. In July 1941 they entered southern French Indochina (modern Vietnam). By mid-1941, the Philippines were threatened on three sides. As diplomatic relations with Japan deteriorated, military and political leaders

DOUGLAS MACARTHUR

After graduating at the top of his class from the U.S. Military Academy at West Point in 1903, Douglas MacArthur served his first posting in the Philippines. His career advanced rapidly. By 1913, he was a member of the U.S. Army's general staff. After World War I, he became superintendent of West Point. He was again posted to the Philippines, but returned to Washington in 1930 to serve as the chief of staff. Although he retired in 1937, MacArthur was recalled in July 1941 to command the U.S. Army Forces in the Far East. Having said that he could defend the Philippines, MacArthur took Japan's invasion as a blow to his integrity. On Corregidor he made it clear that he was willing to fight on. However, the Allies needed a supreme commander in Southeast Asia to organize the fight against the Japanese. Roosevelt ordered MacArthur to leave the Philippines. He left for Australia on March 12, 1942. After a week-long journey, he arrived to tell reporters: "I have come through and I shall return." His men fought on for another two months. "I shall return" became a catchphrase for MacArthur and a public declaration of his zeal to liberate the Philippines, which colored his view of strategic aims throughout the war.

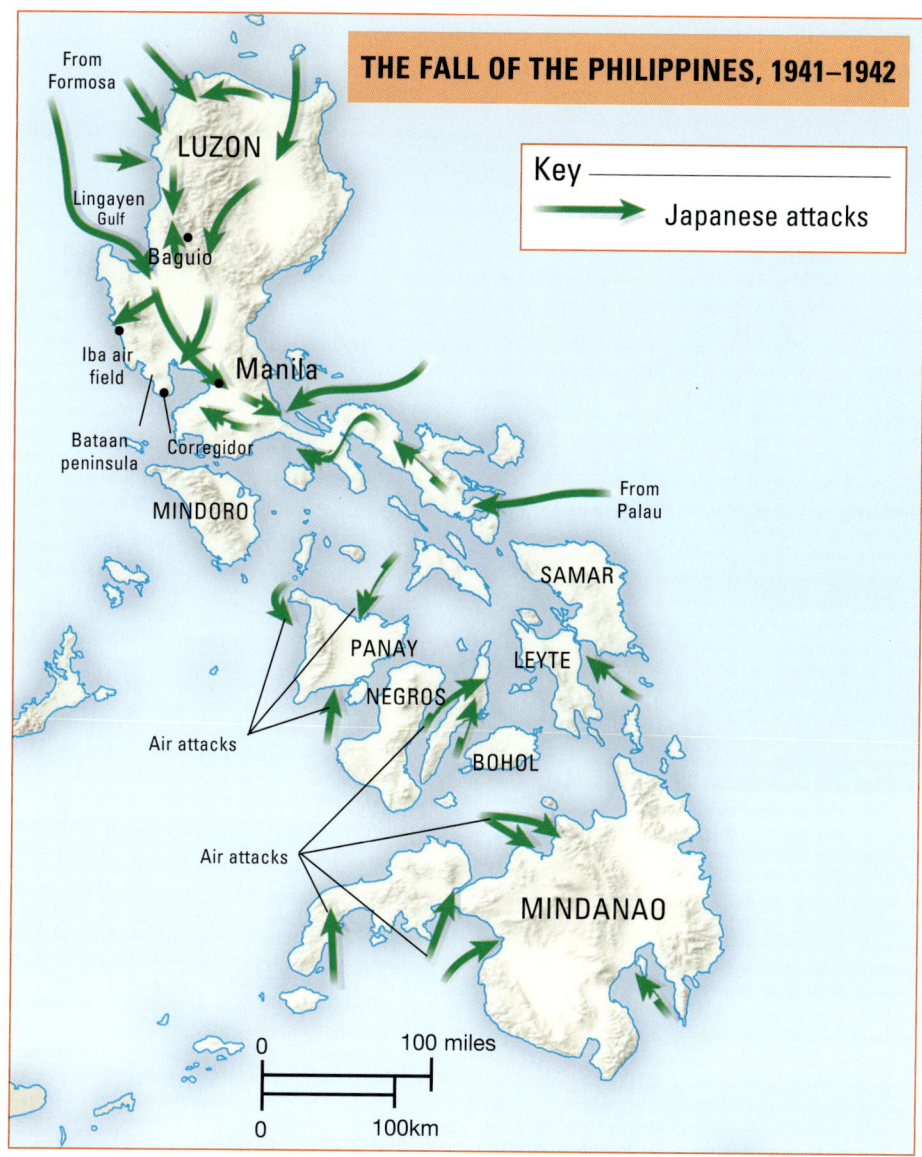

THE FALL OF THE PHILIPPINES, 1941–1942

From Formosa

LUZON

Lingayen Gulf

Baguio

Iba air field

Manila

Bataan peninsula

Corregidor

MINDORO

Key

→ Japanese attacks

From Palau

SAMAR

PANAY

LEYTE

NEGROS

Air attacks

BOHOL

Air attacks

MINDANAO

0 ———— 100 miles

0 ———— 100km

U.S. defense of the Philippines was concentrated around Manila Bay on the northern island of Luzon.

in Washington, D.C., decided to reinforce the Philippines. They rushed to create defenses to counter a Japanese attack that was starting to seem inevitable.

In July 1941, U.S. leaders appointed General Douglas MacArthur to head a new command in the region. It was named U.S. Army Forces in the Far East (USAFFE). MacArthur was a famed but controversial commander who had retired from the U.S. Army. He was in the Philippines acting as a military adviser to the president, Manuel Quezon.

To defend some 115,000 square miles (300,000 sq km) of territory, MacArthur had only 12,000 men of the Philippine Division, 4,000 men of the Philippine Army, and 20,000 Filipino "irregulars," or trained militia. The number of recruits was significantly higher by December.

The Philippine Division was led by General Jonathan Wainwright. It comprised the U.S. Army-trained Philippine Scouts, led by U.S. officers, together with the only U.S. Army unit in the Philippines, the 31st Infantry

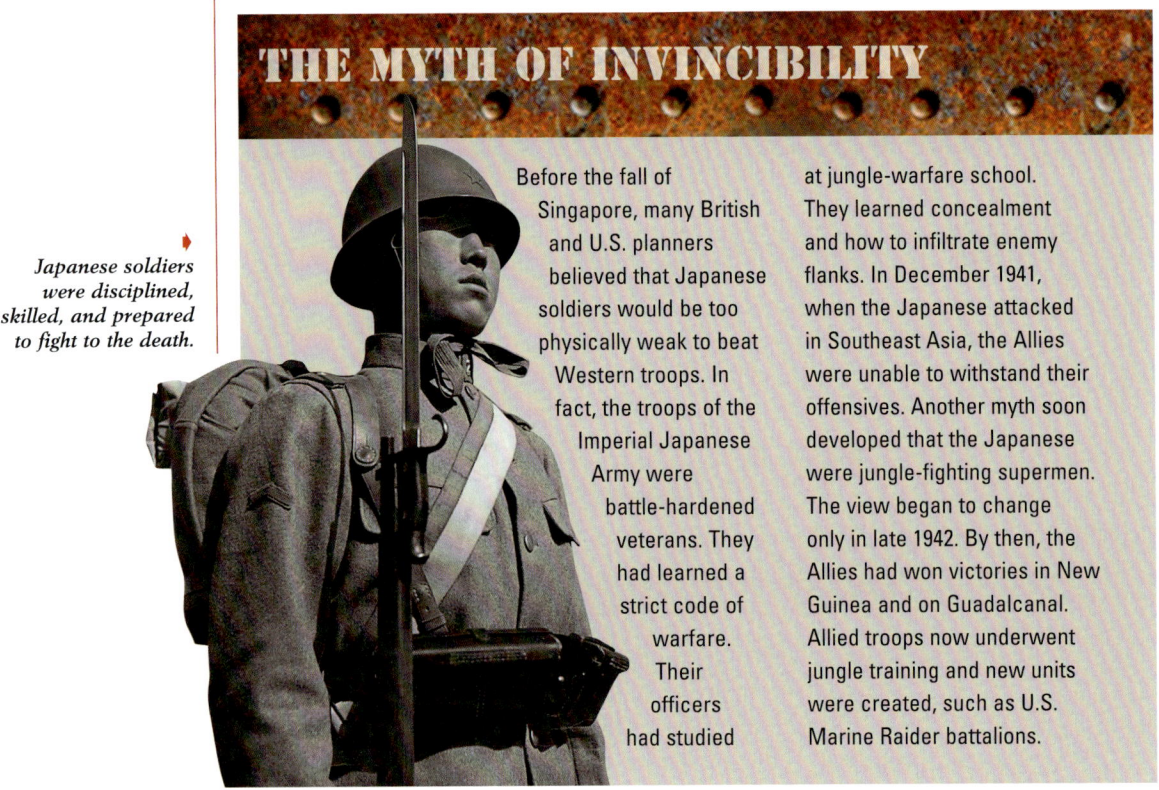

THE MYTH OF INVINCIBILITY

Japanese soldiers were disciplined, skilled, and prepared to fight to the death.

Before the fall of Singapore, many British and U.S. planners believed that Japanese soldiers would be too physically weak to beat Western troops. In fact, the troops of the Imperial Japanese Army were battle-hardened veterans. They had learned a strict code of warfare. Their officers had studied at jungle-warfare school. They learned concealment and how to infiltrate enemy flanks. In December 1941, when the Japanese attacked in Southeast Asia, the Allies were unable to withstand their offensives. Another myth soon developed that the Japanese were jungle-fighting supermen. The view began to change only in late 1942. By then, the Allies had won victories in New Guinea and on Guadalcanal. Allied troops now underwent jungle training and new units were created, such as U.S. Marine Raider battalions.

Regiment, which numbered some 2,100 men.

MacArthur inherited a defense plan for the Philippines known as War Plan Orange. It had last been updated in April 1941. The plan recommended defending only Manila Bay. The U.S. garrison in Manila, the capital, would withdraw to the Bataan Peninsula and the fortified island of Corregidor. The plan reflected Japan's strength and the weakness of the islands' defenses. U.S. military commanders had decided that most of the Philippines would be sacrificed if the Japanese attacked.

War Plan Orange

MacArthur, however, wanted to cancel War Plan Orange. He urged his superiors to adopt an ambitious program to build up the Philippines as a stronghold of U.S. power. MacArthur called for some 200,000 men. Because he had only limited naval resources available, he also called for the creation of a huge air force in the islands. MacArthur wanted hundreds of the new Boeing B-17 bomber, which was later known as the "Flying Fortress." The bombers would to be able to attack Japanese bases on Formosa and any approaching invasion fleet.

Filipino Scouts load a 10-inch gun on a U.S. ship. The U.S.-trained Scouts were key to defending the Philippines.

US chief of staff George C. Marshall gave top priority to reinforcing and equipping USAFFE. MacArthur hoped that the program could be in place by 1942. He did not take into account the logistical problems of building up and supporting large forces so far from the United States, however. A shortage of cargo space on military ships delayed shipments across the Pacific.

The U.S. Far East Air Force

MacArthur's plan to gain air superiority had influential support. Senior officers in the United States Army Air Force (USAAF) were eager to prove the value of high-altitude bombing. By the late summer of 1941, all new U.S. warplanes not earmarked for Britain and Russia in their fight against Germany were scheduled to go to the Philippines. By the middle of 1942, MacArthur

would have four bomber groups of 314 aircraft and two fighter groups of 260 aircraft. The new force, the U.S. Far East Air Force, would be led by General Lewis H. Brereton. He arrived on Luzon in late 1941.

As warplanes arrived on Luzon, however, so warships left. The U.S. Navy's small Asiatic Fleet was dispersed from Luzon south to Mindanao and to Borneo, in the Dutch East Indies, to avoid air attack. The naval presence on Luzon was reduced to a dozen patrol boats, although there were still 29 submarines, 32 patrol aircraft, and the 4th Marine Regiment.

A force to be reckoned with

By December 1941, MacArthur's army had grown in size to more than 19,000 U.S. soldiers and 12,000 Philippine Scouts. A further 100,000

Japanese troops pass through a burned-out Filipino town, one of many settlements wiped out in the fighting to conquer the islands.

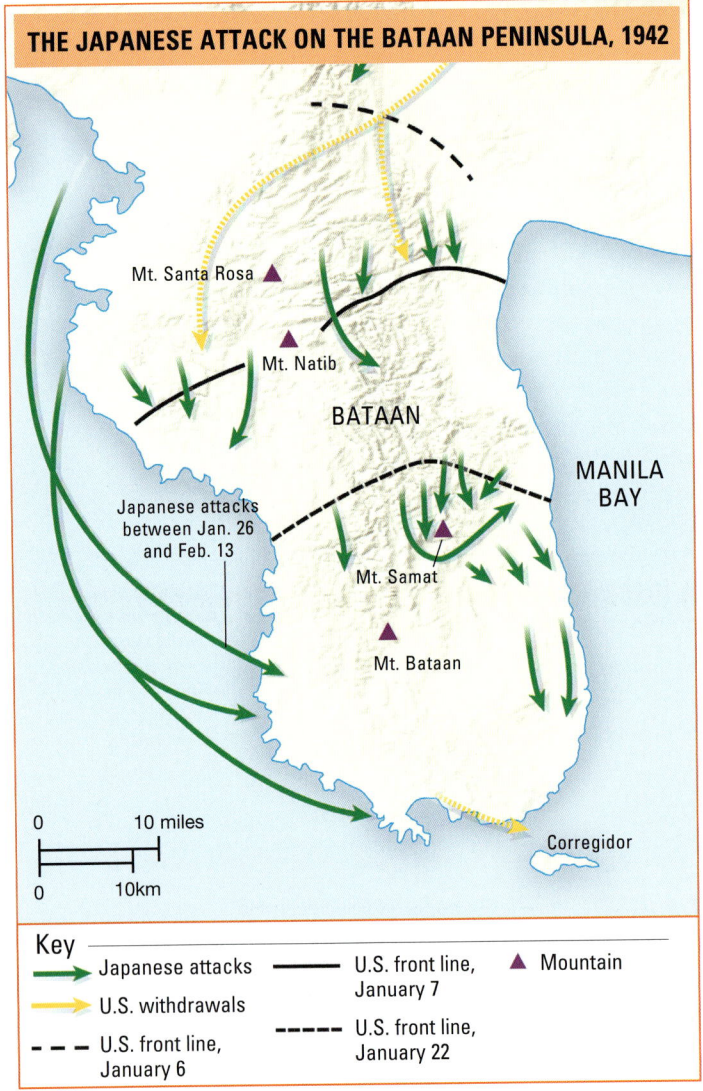

THE JAPANESE ATTACK ON THE BATAAN PENINSULA, 1942

Mt. Santa Rosa ▲

Mt. Natib ▲

BATAAN

MANILA BAY

Japanese attacks between Jan. 26 and Feb. 13

Mt. Samat ▲

Mt. Bataan ▲

0   10 miles

0   10km

Corregidor

Key

→ Japanese attacks
→ U.S. withdrawals
- - - U.S. front line, January 6

—— U.S. front line, January 7
- - - - U.S. front line, January 22
▲ Mountain

The Bataan Peninsula was mountainous and covered with dense jungle. The only escape route was to the tiny fortified island of Corregidor.

and thousands of tons of supplies. The potential of the growing air force was limited, however. The islands lacked airfields and maintenance facilities. They also had poor anti-aircraft defenses. That left aircraft on the ground vulnerable to attack. Despite such problems, MacArthur estimated that he would be able to meet any invasion by summer 1942.

The Japanese prepare to strike

MacArthur did not have that long. By November 1941, the Japanese had moved an invasion force of General Masaharu Homma's Fourteenth Army from China to Formosa. On December 4, a heavily defended convoy left Formosa carrying 43,000 men. Meanwhile, the Japanese had assembled a powerful force of 500 aircraft on Formosa. They planned a surprise attack on Luzon to destroy Brereton's air force on the ground and clear the way for a landing.

The first Japanese air raids were scheduled for dawn on December 8. Given the time difference, that would be only three or four hours after the attack on Pearl Harbor, some 3,000 miles (4,800 km) away. However, heavy fog over Formosa prevented the aircraft from taking off.

Devastating aerial attack

By 03:30 hours, news of the attack on Pearl Harbor had reached MacArthur. He ordered his troops to battle stations. It was only much later in the morning that he sent a reconnaissance flight to Formosa, however. By the time he authorized a bombing raid on the Japanese bases at lunchtime, it was too late. The fog over Formosa had cleared hours earlier. Some 200 Japanese war-planes were now approaching the B-17 base at Clark Field, 75 miles (120km) north of Manila.

Filipino militia were under training. MacArthur organized his troops in four groups: Northern Luzon Forces, under Wainwright; Southern Luzon Forces, under General George Parker; a Reserve Force to protect Manila; and a force to defend the southern Philippines.

MacArthur's air force now had about 270 aircraft. They included 100 modern Curtiss P-40 Warhawk fighters and 35 B-17s. He was expecting 128 more bombers by February. A convoy was also due to bring another 70 fighters, an artillery brigade, hundreds of vehicles,

The Japanese caught 18 U.S. B-17s on the gound and a number of P-40 fighters just taking off. Within an hour, they had destroyed all the B-17s and more than half of the P-40s. Elsewhere the Japanese launched air raids against Iba Field in northwest Luzon; Baguio, the so-called summer capital of the Philippines; and Mindanao. By the end of the day, the U.S. Far East Air Force had lost half of its aircraft.

Japanese raids began again next day. Within 24 hours they had destroyed seven more airfields and a naval base. Brereton withdrew his remaining B-17s to Mindanao to organize attacks on Japanese convoys off Luzon's northern coast.

Japanese troop landings

That same day, Japanese troops landed on the north and northwest coasts of Luzon. They were small forces sent to capture airfields, but their effect on the militia was devastating: the Filipinos fell back in confusion. Their retreat ended MacArthur's hope of defeating the Japanese on the beaches.

The main Japanese landing took place on December 22. Homma's 48th Division came ashore at Lingayen Gulf, 120 miles (195 km) northwest of Manila. Striking inland, it cut off the northern part of Luzon and began to advance on Manila and Bataan.

Withdrawal to Bataan

MacArthur ordered his troops to withdraw into Bataan. On December 23, a second Japanese division landed at Lamon Bay, south of Manila. It advanced north. MacArthur's forces were now cut off on two sides.

Communications began to collapse as U.S. and Filipino units streamed back toward the Bataan Peninsula. The command structure was kept in place by Wainwright and the commander of the Southern Luzon Force, George Parker. Parker fought a staged withdrawal. Homma held off some of his forces, because he thought he would have to fight for Manila. Instead, on December 26, MacArthur declared Manila an open city to save it from attack. He moved his headquarters onto the island of Corregidor and told his commanders that Plan Orange was now in effect.

A landing craft full of Japanese soldiers approaches the burning city of Manila late in December 1941.

The Japanese entered Manila on January 2, 1942. On January 5, U.S. and Filippino forces completed their withdrawal into Bataan. About 80,000 troops and more than 25,000 civilians were trapped on a mountainous peninsula covered in jungle. Bataan was 14 miles (22 km) wide and 30 miles (45 km) long. It had no escape route.

In their rapid withdrawal, U.S. and Filipino troops had left behind most of their equipment. They had very limited supplies in Bataan. As a result of MacArthur's plan to defend all of the Philippines, food, ammunition, weapons, and medical supplies were widely dispersed. United States and Filipino

troops in Bataan were on half-rations; within weeks they were eating mules.

United States and Filipino forces set up defenses across the neck of the peninsula. The west was defended by I Corps under Wainwright and the east was held by II Corps under Parker. Between them lay Mount Natib, over 4,000 feet (1,220 m) high. A second line was set up 8 miles (13 km) south, in front of two more high points.

Japanese forces were weakened after their advance. Homma had suffered nearly 7,000 casualties and a malaria epidemic had left 13,000 men sick. A division had also been transferred to the Dutch East Indies. He was reinforced

Wearing British-syle helmets that were replaced later in the war, U.S. troops survey the damage caused by a Japanese air raid on the Philippine town of Paranaque in December 1941.

BATAAN DEATH MARCH

The Japanese took more than 12,000 American and 60,000 Filipino prisoners on Bataan. They were to be held at a camp more than 100 miles (160 km) north. The Allies had been on starvation rations for months. They were exhausted and sick from malaria and dysentery. The Japanese forced them to march all day, without food or water, in 95°F (35°C) heat. Prisoners who fell behind were executed. What became known as the Bataan Death March began on April 10 and lasted a week.

The survivors were packed into airless railcars for an eight-hour journey. They were then marched another 8 miles (13km) to the camp. Of the 72,000 prisoners, some 18,000 died. General Homma, the Japanese commander who ordered the march, was arrested after the war. He was tried, found guilty of murder, and executed in April 1946.

American prisoners leaving Bataan carry sick comrades in improvised stretchers.

by only one inexperienced brigade. Still, Homma launched his first attack on Bataan on January 9. He had promised that he could conquer the Philippines in 45 days. He would lose face if his campaign stalled.

The campaign for Bataan

MacArthur remained confident that his troops could hold out. On January 10, he left Corregidor to inspect the Bataan defenses. It was his only visit to the peninsula: his preference for staying on Corregidor led his troops to nickname him "Dugout Doug."

The first line of U.S. defenses held until January 15, when the Japanese found a route over Mount Natib. They attacked the flank of Parker's II Corps. They then infiltrated Wainwright's position from behind. The U.S. forces withdrew to the second defensive line on January 22. At the same time, Homma attempted three amphibious landings on the west coast of the peninsula behind the U.S. and Filipino positions. All three landings were thrown back with heavy losses.

Japanese progress

The second defensive line held, but by the end of February the Bataan defenders were on starvation rations. Most were suffering from malnutrition, malaria, or dysentery. The U.S. government told MacArthur that his troops could not be rescued. Neither could they surrender, however. The government wanted to show a sign of U.S. determination to fight. At the same

A Japanese assault team uses a flame thrower against a U.S. position during the attack on Corregidor.

time, it did not want to risk having such an important commander as MacArthur captured by the enemy. He was evacuated to Australia on March 12, making a famous promise to the Filipinos: "I shall return." Wainwright took command of U.S. forces in the Philippines.

Meanwhile Homma received two new divisions of troops. His strengthened forces launched a fresh attack on April 3. Exhausted, the defenders finally broke. Wainwright withdrew to Corregidor to organize what few defenses remained in the Philippines. He left General Edward King to hold out as long as he could in Bataan. On April 9, despite a radio call from MacArthur ordering Wainwright to launch a counterattack, King accepted the hopelessness of the situation and surrendered his forces.

Corregidor stands alone

Corregidor now stood alone in the Philippines. Survivors from Bataan had increased its garrison to more than 11,000. Water, food, and medical supplies were running out. Homma could have waited and starved the defenders into submission. His pride drove him to take the island by force, however. Corregidor had been under air attack since the end of March. Homma now ordered an artillery bombardment from Bataan. On May 1, a huge artillery barrage wrecked what few defensive positions were left on the surface. Only underground defenses remained. During the night of May 3/4, a U.S. submarine arrived to remove the last evacuees.

Wainwright stayed on Corregidor. Early on May 6, Japanese troops and three tanks landed on the eastern end of the island. The fighting moved west, around the entrance to the Malinta Tunnel, the U.S. headquarters. The defenders held the Japanese back until midday. Wainwright was concerned for the 1,000 wounded in the Malinta Tunnel. He surrendered.

Homma forced Wainwright to order all U.S. and Filipino forces in the islands to surrender. He threatened to kill the Corregidor garrison if he did not. On May 8, Wainwright broadcast the order across the Philippines. It was a humiliating end to a brave defense.

Japanese soldiers celebrate their conquest of the Philippine islands in April 1942.

SEPTEMBER 1

POLAND

A German force of 53 divisions, supported by 1,600 aircraft, crosses the German and Slovak borders into Poland in a pincer movement. World War II has begun.

SEPTEMBER 3

BRITAIN AND FRANCE

Britain and France declare war on Nazi Germany after the Nazis ignore their demands to immediately withdraw from Poland.

SEPTEMBER 9

POLAND

A Polish counterattack is launched over the Bzura River against Germany's Eighth Army. It only achieves short-term success. The Polish Army is rapidly falling to pieces under the relentless German attacks.

SEPTEMBER 17–30

POLAND

In accordance with a secret pact with Germany, the Soviet Red Army invades Poland. Little resistance is encountered on Poland's eastern border as the Polish Army is fighting for its life to the west.

SEPTEMBER 18–30

POLAND

Poland is defeated and split into two zones of occupation divided by the Bug River. Germany has lost 10,572 troops and the Soviet Union has 734 men killed in the campaign. Around 50,000 Poles are killed and 750,000 captured.

SEPTEMBER 29

SOVIET UNION

After occupying Poland, the Soviet Union concentrates on extending its control over the Baltic Sea region. During the next few weeks it gains bases and signs "mutual assistance" agreements with Lithuania, Latvia, and Estonia. Finland, however, will not agree to the Soviet Union's demands and prepares to fight.

OCTOBER 14

SEA WAR, NORTH SEA

The British battleship *Royal Oak* is sunk, with 786 lives lost, after *U-47* passes through antisubmarine defenses at Scapa Flow in the Orkneys.

NOVEMBER 30

EASTERN FRONT, FINLAND

A Soviet army of over 600,000 men, backed by air and naval power, attacks Finland. Highly-motivated Finnish troops use their familiarity with the terrain and use their ability to ski through snow-covered areas to launch hit-and-run raids on Red Army units bogged down in the snow.

DECEMBER 16

FINLAND

The Red Army begins a major new offensive. To compensate for their lack of armor and artillery, the Finns use improvised explosive devices ("Molotov Cocktails," named after the Soviet foreign minister) to destroy enemy tanks.

DECEMBER 13

ATLANTIC OCEAN

British ships fight the German pocket battleship *Graf Spee* at Battle of the River Plate. The *Graf Spee* is scuttled by its crew on the 17th.

1940

MARCH 11

FINLAND

The Treaty of Moscow between Finland and the Soviet Union is agreed, ending the Winter War. Finland retains its independence but has to surrender the Karelian Isthmus and Hangö – 10 percent of its territory. Campaign losses: 200,000 Soviet troops and 25,000 Finns.

APRIL 9

NORWAY/DENMARK

A German invasion force, including surface ships, U-boats, and 1,000 aircraft, attacks Denmark and Norway. Denmark is overrun immediately.

APRIL 14–19

NORWAY

An Allied expeditionary force of over 10,000 British, French, and Polish troops lands in Norway.

MAY 7–10

BRITAIN

Prime Minister Neville Chamberlain is severely criticized over the Norwegian campaign. He resigns and is replaced by Winston Churchill.

MAY 10

THE LOW COUNTRIES

German forces invade the Low Countries. But the main German attack will take place in the south, in the Ardennes region of France.

MAY 12–14

FRANCE

German forces reach the Meuse River and fight their way across at Sedan and Dinant on the 13th. German armor advances westward rapidly, opening a 50-mile (75-km) gap in the Allied line. Allied units retreat to the Channel port of Dunkirk.

MAY 26

FRANCE/BELGIUM

Operation Dynamo, the evacuation of Allied forces from the Dunkirk area, begins using small boats and naval vessels.

MAY 31

UNITED STATES

President Franklin D. Roosevelt launches a "billion-dollar defense program" to bolster the armed forces.

JUNE 1–9

NORWAY

After Britain and France reveal to the Norwegians that they are to begin an evacuation, troops begin to withdraw. King Haakon orders his Norwegians to stop fighting on June 9.

June 3–4
FRANCE
Operation Dynamo ends. The remarkable operation has rescued 338,226 men—two-thirds of them British—from the Dunkirk beaches.

June 16–24
FRANCE
Marshal Henri-Philippe Pétain, the new French president, requests an armistice on the 17th. It is agreed on the 22nd. Germany occupies two-thirds of France, including the Channel and Atlantic coastlines.

July 1
ATLANTIC OCEAN
The "Happy Time" begins for U-boat crews as their range is increased now that they have bases in French ports. This lasts until October. U-boat crews inflict serious losses on Allied convoys.

July 10
BRITAIN
The Battle of Britain begins. Hermann Göring, the Nazi air force chief, orders attacks on shipping and ports in the English Channel.

July 21
SOVIET UNION
The Soviets annex Lithuania, Latvia, and Estonia.

August 24–25
BRITAIN
The Luftwaffe inflicts serious losses on the Royal Air Force (RAF) during attacks on its main air bases in southeast England, straining the resources of Fighter Command to breaking point in a few days.

August 26–29
GERMANY
The RAF launches a night raid with 81 aircraft on Berlin following a similar raid on London. Hitler is outraged and vows revenge. German aircraft are redirected to make retaliatory raids on London. This relieves the pressure on Fighter Command's air bases.

September 7–30
AIR WAR, BRITAIN
Full-scale bombing raids on London—the "Blitz"—begin with 500 bombers and 600 fighters.

October 28
GREECE
Italy attacks Greece from Albania. The winter weather limits air support and thousands die of cold.

November 5
UNITED STATES
President Franklin D. Roosevelt is elected for a third term.

November 11–12
MEDITERRANEAN
At the Battle of Taranto, British torpedo aircraft from the carrier *Illustrious* destroy three Italian battleships and damage two other vessels during the raid on the Italian base.

December 9–11
EGYPT
The British launch their first offensive in the Western Desert. The Western Desert Force (31,000) attacks the fortified camps that have been established by the Italians in Egypt. Some 34,000 Italians are taken prisoner as they retreat rapidly from Egypt.

1941

January 2
POLITICS, UNITED STATES
President Franklin D. Roosevelt announces a program to produce 200 freighters—"Liberty" ships—to support the Allied Atlantic convoys.

February 14
NORTH AFRICA
To aid the faltering Italians, the first units of General Erwin Rommel's Afrika Korps land at Tripoli.

March 11
UNITED STATES
President Franklin D. Roosevelt signs the Lend-Lease Act that allows Britain to obtain supplies without having to immediately pay for them in cash.

April 6–15
YUGOSLAVIA/GREECE
Thirty-three German divisions, with Italian and Hungarian support, invade Yugoslavia from the north, east, and southeast. German forces also attack Greece from the north.

April 17
YUGOSLAVIA
Yugoslavia surrenders to Germany. Immediately, guerrilla forces emerge to resist the Nazi occupation.

April 27
GREECE
German forces occupy Athens. Campaign dead: Greek 15,700; Italian 13,755; German 1,518; and British 900.

May 20–22
CRETE
A German force of 23,000 men, supported by 600 aircraft, attacks Crete. The Germans launch the first major airborne operation in history.

May 23–27
ATLANTIC OCEAN
British ships find the German battleship *Bismarck* and cruiser *Prinz Eugen* in the Denmark Straits between Iceland and Greenland. The *Bismarck* sinks the cruiser *Hood* and damages the battleship *Prince of Wales*, but is then sunk.

May 28–31
CRETE
Crete falls to the Germans. British losses are 1,742 men, plus 2,011 dead and wounded at sea, while Germany has 3,985 men killed.

June 22
SOVIET UNION
Germany launches Operation Barbarossa, the invasion of the Soviet Union, with three million men divided into three army groups along a 2000-mile (3200-km) front. Army Group North strikes toward the Baltic and Leningrad. Army Group Center aims to take Smolensk and then Moscow. Army Group South advances toward the Ukraine and the Caucasus.

July 31
GERMANY
Reinhard Heydrich, Germany's security chief and head of the SS secret police, receives orders to begin creating a draft plan for the murder of the Jews, which becomes known as the "Final Solution."

September 30
SOVIET UNION
Operation Typhoon, the German attack on Moscow, officially begins.

NOVEMBER 26
PACIFIC OCEAN
The Japanese First Air Fleet leaves the Kurile Islands on a mission to destroy the U.S. Pacific Fleet at Pearl Harbor, Hawaii.

DECEMBER 7
HAWAII
The Japanese attack Pearl Harbor. Over 183 Japanese aircraft destroy six battleships and 188 aircraft, damage or sink 10 other vessels, and kill 2,000 servicemen. The Japanese lose 29 aircraft.

DECEMBER 8
SOVIET UNION
Adolf Hitler reluctantly agrees to suspend the advance on Moscow for the duration of the winter.

DECEMBER 11
AXIS
Germany and Italy declare war on the United States.

1942

JANUARY 10–11
DUTCH EAST INDIES
A Japanese force begins attacking the Dutch East Indies to secure the oil assets of this island-chain.

JANUARY 20
GERMANY
At the Wannsee Conference, Berlin, deputy head of the SS Reinhard Heydrich reveals his plans for the "Final Solution" to the so-called Jewish problem. Heydrich receives permission to begin deporting all Jews in German-controlled areas to Eastern Europe to face either forced labor or extermination.

FEBRUARY 8–14
SINGAPORE
Japanese troops capture Singapore. Japan has fewer than 10,000 casualties in Malaya. British forces have lost 138,000 men.

APRIL 9
PHILIPPINES
Major General Jonathan Wainright, commanding the U.S. and Filipino forces, surrenders to the Japanese.

APRIL 18
JAPAN
Lieutenant Colonel James Doolittle leads 16 B-25 bombers, launched from the carrier *Hornet*, against targets in Japan, including Tokyo.

JUNE 4
PACIFIC OCEAN
The Battle of Midway begins. Japan's Admiral Chuichi Nagumo aims to seize the U.S. base at Midway and then destroy the U.S. Pacific Fleet. Japan deploys 165 vessels, including eight carriers. The U.S. Navy has a smaller force but has three carriers. The loss of half of its carrier strength in the battle, plus 275 aircraft, puts Japan on the defensive in the Pacific.

JUNE 21
LIBYA
Following the Allied withdrawal into Egypt, the Tobruk garrison falls following German land and air attacks.

JUNE 28
SOVIET UNION
Germany launches its summer offensive, Operation Blue, with its Army Group South attacking east from Kursk toward Voronezh.

JULY 4–10
SOVIET UNION
The siege of Sevastopol ends with the Germans capturing 90,000 men.

AUGUST 7–21
GUADALCANAL
The U.S. 1st Marine Division lands on Guadalcanal Island to overwhelm the Japanese garrison.

SEPTEMBER 2
POLAND
The Nazis are "clearing" the Jewish Warsaw Ghetto. Over 50,000 Jews have been killed by poison gas or sent to concentration camps.

OCTOBER 23
EGYPT
The Battle of El Alamein begins. An attack by 195,000 Allied troops against 104,000 Axis men begins.

NOVEMBER 2–24
EGYPT / LIBYA
Rommel, severely lacking supplies, decides to withdraw from El Alamein.

Germany and Italy have lost 59,000 men killed, wounded, or captured. The Allies have suffered 13,000 killed, wounded, or missing.

NOVEMBER 19
SOVIET UNION
General Zhukov launches a Soviet counteroffensive at Stalingrad to trap the Germans in a massive pincer movement.

1943

FEBRUARY 2
SOVIET UNION
The siege of Stalingrad ends. Field Marshal Friedrich Paulus and 93,000 German troops surrender.

FEBRUARY 14–22
TUNISIA
In the Battle of Kasserine Pass, Rommel's forces cause panic among U.S. troops. He loses 2,000 men; the Americans 10,000.

APRIL 17
GERMANY
The U.S. Eighth Army Air Force attacks Bremen's aircraft factories from its bases in eastern England. Sixteen of the 115 B-17 Flying Fortress bombers from the raid are lost.

MAY 13
TUNISIA
Axis forces surrender. Some 620,000 casualties and prisoners have been sustained by Germany and Italy. Allied campaign losses: French 20,000; British 19,000; and U.S. 18,500.

JULY 5
SOVIET UNION
Over 6000 German and Soviet tanks and assault guns take part in the Battle of Kursk.

JULY 9
SICILY
U.S. and British troops begin the attack on Sicily.

JULY 12–13
SOVIET UNION
At Kursk, the Soviets launch a counter-offensive around Prokhorovka and an enormous tank battle develops. The German offensive is defeated.

AUGUST 11–17

SICILY
The Germans finally start withdrawing before U.S. forces enter Messina on the 17th.

SEPTEMBER 9

ITALY
Lieutenant General Mark Clark's U.S. Fifth Army, plus the British X Corps, lands in the Gulf of Salerno.

SEPTEMBER 25

SOVIET UNION
The Soviets recapture Smolensk in their continuing offensive. Germany's Army Group Center is now falling back in some disarray.

NOVEMBER 6

SOVIET UNION
The Soviets recapture Kiev.

DECEMBER 26

ARCTIC OCEAN
At the Battle of the North Cape, the German battleship *Scharnhorst* is sunk.

1944

JANUARY 14–27

SOVIET UNION
The Red Army ends the German blockade of Leningrad. Some 830,000 civilians have died during the siege.

JANUARY 22

ITALY
Troops of the Allied VI Corps make an amphibious landing at Anzio, behind the German lines.

MARCH 7–8

BURMA / INDIA
Operation U-Go, the Japanese offensive to drive the Allies back into India by destroying their bases at Imphal and Kohima, begins.

MARCH 20–22

ITALY
Despite further frontal attacks by New Zealand troops, the German defenders repulse all efforts to dislodge them from Monte Cassino.

MAY 18

ITALY
The Allies capture the monastery of Monte Cassino.

JUNE 6

FRANCE
The Allies launch the greatest amphibious operation in military history—D-Day. Some 50,000 men land on five invasion beaches to establish a toehold in Normandy. Allied casualties are 2,500 dead.

JUNE 19–21

PHILIPPINE SEA
Battle of the Philippine Sea. Japan's Combined Fleet is defeated by the U.S. Fifth Fleet. The Japanese lose 346 aircraft and two carriers. U.S. losses are 30 aircraft and slight damage to a battleship.

JUNE 22

SOVIET UNION
The Red Army launches Operation Bagration against Germany's Army Group Center.

JULY 20

GERMANY
An attempt is made by German officers to assassinate Adolf Hitler. It fails to kill the Führer.

AUGUST 1

POLAND
The Warsaw uprising begins. Some 38,000 soldiers of the Polish Home Army battle with about the same number of German troops.

AUGUST 25

FRANCE
The commander of the German garrison of Paris, General Dietrich von Choltitz, surrenders to the Allies.

SEPTEMBER 17

HOLLAND
Operation Market Garden, an Allied armored and airborne thrust across Holland to outflank the German defenses, begins. Paratroopers land at Arnhem, Eindhoven, and Nijmegen to capture vital bridges.

SEPTEMBER 22–25

HOLLAND
The paratroopers fall back from Arnhem, leaving 2,500 dead behind.

OCTOBER 2

POLAND
The last Poles in Warsaw surrender as the Germans crush the uprising. Polish

deaths number 150,000. The Germans have lost 26,000 men.

OCTOBER 20

PHILIPPINES
As the U.S. Sixth Army lands on Leyte Island, General Douglas MacArthur wades ashore and keeps a promise he made two years earlier: "I shall return."

OCTOBER 23–26

PHILIPPINES
Following the U.S. landings on Leyte, the Japanese Combined Fleet is defeated at the Battle of Leyte Gulf.

DECEMBER 16–22

BELGIUM
Hitler launches Operation Watch on the Rhine, his attempt to capture Antwerp. The thick fog means the Germans achieve complete surprise. But they fail to capture Bastogne.

1945

JANUARY 9

PHILIPPINES
The U.S. Sixth Army makes unopposed amphibious landings on Luzon.

JANUARY 27

POLAND
The Red Army liberates the Nazi death camp at Auschwitz.

JANUARY 28

BELGIUM
The last bits of the German "bulge" in the Ardennes are wiped out. The Germans have lost 100,000 killed, wounded, and captured in their defeat. The Americans have lost 81,000 killed, wounded, or captured, and the British 1,400 killed.

JANUARY 30

GERMANY
The Red Army is only 100 miles (160 km) from Berlin.

FEBRUARY 4–11

SOVIET UNION
Marshal Joseph Stalin, President Franklin D. Roosevelt, and Prime Minister Winston Churchill meet at the Yalta Conference in the Crimea to discuss postwar Europe. The "Big Three" decide that Germany will be divided into four zones, administered

by Britain, France, the United States, and the Soviet Union.

FEBRUARY 13–14
GERMANY
The RAF mounts a night raid on Dresden. The 805 bombers inflict massive damage on the city, killing 50,000 people.

FEBRUARY 17
IWO JIMA
Under the command of Lieutenant General Holland M. Smith, the U.S. Marines land on the island of Iwo Jima. The attackers are hit by intense artillery and small-arms fire from the 21,000-man Japanese garrison.

MARCH 16
IWO JIMA
The island of Iwo Jima is declared secure by the Americanst. They have lost 6,821 soldiers and sailors dead, while of the 21,000 Japanese garrison, only 1,083 are taken prisoner.

MARCH 22–31
GERMANY
The Allied crossings of the Rhine River begin. German resistance is negligible.

APRIL 1
OKINAWA
Operation Iceberg, the U.S. invasion of the island, commences. The island, only 325 miles (520 km) from Japan, has two airfields on the western side and two partially-protected bays on the east coast—an excellent springboard for the proposed invasion of the Japanese mainland.

APRIL 7
PACIFIC OCEAN
The Japanese *Yamato*, the world's largest battleship, is sunk at sea during an attack by U.S. warplanes.

APRIL 9
ITALY
The final campaign in Italy begins as the U.S. Fifth and British Eighth Armies attack the Germans.

APRIL 12
UNITED STATES
President Franklin D. Roosevelt dies of a cerebral hemorrhage. Vice President Harry S. Truman takes over the position of president.

APRIL 16
GERMANY
The Soviet offensive to capture Berlin commences with a total of 2.5 million men, 41,600 guns and mortars, 6,250 tanks and self-propelled guns, and 7,500 combat aircraft. The Germans have one million men, 10,400 guns and mortars, 1,500 tanks or assault guns, and 3,300 combat aircraft.

APRIL 27
GERMANY
"Fortress Berlin" has been reduced to an east-to-west belt 10 miles (16 km) long by three miles (5 km) wide. German forces within the city are affected by widespread desertions and suicides.

APRIL 28
ITALY
Former Italian dictator Benitto Mussolini and his mistress Claretta Petacci are captured by partisans. They are both shot.

APRIL 30
GERMANY
Adolf Hitler and Eva Braun commit suicide in the Führerbunker in Berlin.

MAY 2
GERMANY
Following a savage three-day battle, in which half the garrison has been killed, Berlin, the capital of Nazi Germany, falls to the Red Army.

MAY 3
BURMA
Following 38 months of Japanese occupation, Rangoon falls to the Allies without a fight.

JUNE 22
OKINAWA
All Japanese resistance on the island ends. The Japanese have lost 110,00 killed during the fighting. The U.S. Tenth Army has suffered 7,613 men killed or missing, and 31,807 wounded.

JULY 17–AUGUST 2
GERMANY
The Potsdam Conference takes place in Berlin. The "Big Three"—U.S. President Harry Truman, Soviet leader Marshal Joseph Stalin, and British Prime Minister Clement Attlee (who had defeated Churchill in a general election on July 5)—meet to discuss postwar

policy. Japan is informed that an immediate surrender would result in the continued existence of its nation, but further resistance will lead to the "utter devastation of the Japanese homeland." This is a veiled reference to the use of atomic weapons against Japan itself.

AUGUST 6
JAPAN
The B-29 Superfortress *Enola Gay* drops an atomic bomb on the Japanese city of Hiroshima, killing 70,000 people and wounding 100,000.

AUGUST 9
MANCHURIA
A massive Soviet offensive by 1.5 million men begins against the Japanese Kwantung Army.

AUGUST 9
JAPAN
A second U.S. atomic bomb is dropped on Nagasaki. It kills 35,000 people and injures a further 60,000.

AUGUST 10
JAPAN
Following a conference, during which the emperor voices his support for an immediate acceptance of the Potsdam Proclamation, Japan announces its willingness to surrender unconditionally.

AUGUST 23
MANCHURIA
The campaign in Manchuria ends in total Soviet victory. The Japanese have lost over 80,000 dead and 594,000 taken prisoner. Soviet losses are 8,000 men killed and 22,000 wounded. The Kwantung Army has been destroyed.

SEPTEMBER 2
ALLIES
Aboard the battleship *Missouri* in Tokyo Bay, Japanese officials sign the Instrument of Surrender, bringing World War II to a close.

GLOSSARY

advance A move forward by a military force.

Allies One of the two groups of combatants in the war. The main Allies were Britain, the Soviet Union, the United States, British Empire troops, and free forces from occupied nations.

amphibious An operation that involves actions on water and on land, such as a landing on an island from the sea.

anchorage An area on a coastline that is suitable for large ships to anchor safely.

annex To seize territory and make it part of one's own country.

armor A term referring to armored vehicles, such as tanks.

atrocity A war crime that is particularly cruel or wicked.

battleship The largest and most heavily armed type of warship.

colony A country governed by another country.

dive bomber A war plane that dives toward its target before releasing its bombs at low altitude.

division An army unit made up of 15,000 to 20,000 soldiers.

embargo An order to temporarily stop something, especially trading.

garrison A group of troops placed to defend a location.

imperial A word that describes something related to an empire.

infantry Soldiers who fight on foot, or in vehicles.

isolation A policy that is based on not becoming involved in the affairs of foreign countries.

League of Nations An organization set up after World War I (1914–1918) to settle international disputes without conflict.

militarist A person who advocates a military organization of society and a warlike approach to foreign countries.

militia An irregular army formed by civilian soldiers.

Nationalists A Chinese political group trying to establish government of China by Chinese.

occupation The seizure and control of an area by military force.

offensive A planned military attack.

open city A city that is not defended in the face of a military advance, in order to try to avoid great physical damage or high numbers of casualties.

peninsula A narrow piece of land that projects into a body of water.

perimeter The defended edge of an area of territory.

strategy A detailed plan for achieving success.

strongpoint Any defensive position that has been strengthened to withstand an attack.

treaty A formal agreement between two or more countries.

troops Groups of soldiers.

ultimatum A demand made by one country on another.

veteran A member of the armed services who has experience of being in conflict.

FURTHER READING

»»»» BOOKS

Adams, Simon. *World War II* (Eyewitness Books). Dorling Kindersley, 2007.

Allen, Thomas B. *Remember Pearl Harbor: American and Japanese Survivors Tell Their Stories*. National Geographic Children's Books, 2007.

Davenport, John. *The Attack on Pearl Harbor: The United States Enters World War II* (Milestones in American History). Chelsea House Publishers, 2008.

Dougherty, Steve. *Pearl Harbor: The U.S. Enters World War II* (24/7 Goes to War: On the Battlefield). Scholastic Library Publishing, 2009.

Gorman, Jaqueline Laks. *Pearl Harbor: A Primary Source History* (In Their Own Words). Gareth Stevens Publishing, 2009.

Grant, Reg. *World War II* (DK Readers). DK Children, 2008.

Hamen, Susan E. *Pearl Harbor* (Essential Events). Abdo Publishing Company, 2009.

Haugen, Brenda. *Douglas MacArthur: America's General*. Signature Lives, 2005.

Lassieur, Allison. *The Attack on Pearl Harbor: An Interactive History Adventure* (You Chose Books). Capstone Press, 2008.

Mullener, Elizabeth. *War Stories: Remembering World War II*. Louisiana State University Press, 2004.

Panchyk, Richard. *World War II for Kids: A History With 21 Activities*. Chicago Review Press, 2002.

Samuels, Charlie. *Timeline of World War II: Pacific* (Americans at War). Gareth Stevens Publishing, 2011.

Somervill, Barbara. *Samuria, Shoguns, and Soldiers: The Rise of the Japanese Military* (Lucent Library of Historical Eras). Lucent Books, 2007.

Stein, R. Conrad. *World War II in the Pacific: From Pearl Harbor to Nagasaki* (The United States at War). Enslow Publishing, Inc, 2011.

Wukowitz, John. *Bombing of Pearl Harbor* (World History). Lucent Books, 2011.

»»»» WEB SITES

Due to the changing nature of Internet links, Rosen Publishing has developed an online list of Web sites related to the subject of this book. This site is updated regularly. Please use this link to access the list:

http://www.rosenlinks.com/WW2/Pearl

INDEX